The Success Stories of People Who Stammer (PWS)

Sky is the Limit

V. MANIMARAN

J. AGNEE RAJ

INDIA • SINGAPORE • MALAYSIA

Copyright © J. Agnee Raj 2025
All Rights Reserved.

ISBN
Paperback 979-8-89929-305-4
Hardcase 979-8-89961-642-6

Dedication

This book is dedicated to all the members of the Super Speakers
Group. Without their cooperation, the publication of this book
would not have been possible

CONTENTS

ABOUT THIS BOOK...

Although the title of this book is *"Success Stories of People Who Stammer,"* there are significant differences between the individuals featured in these stories and other people who stammer but haven't made any efforts toward improvement. While the people in these stories may still stammer occasionally, they speak with courage, without fear, shame, or hesitation.

On the other hand, many people who stammer are afraid to speak with others. In speaking situations, they may choose to remain silent. They hesitate to talk openly about their stammering. They believe that stammering is a significant obstacle to their progress. They think they can only move forward after completely overcoming their stammering.

But stammering is a mysterious condition. Is it a disability or a disease? How can it be cured? Is it completely curable? Which is the right path to improvement? How long will it take to speak fluently? There are no clear, definitive answers to these questions. To this day, no one can confidently say what exactly causes stammering. Therefore, there is no one-size-fits-all treatment for it.

Because of this uncertainty, fake speech trainers exploit people by falsely claiming they can cure stammering within a few weeks or months, extracting vast sums of money from them. When the stammering does not go away within the promised time, and the affected person questions the trainer, these frauds blame the individual, saying they didn't follow the methods correctly. But the truth is, no person who stammers can speak exactly as those trainers suggest.

So, how did these 40 people with stammering succeed in life?

Do they all now speak fluently?

Did they all follow the same method?

Or did each one take a unique approach?

How did each of them achieve success?

Moreover, it is admirable that all 40 individuals featured in this book bravely shared not only their real stories but also their true names and email addresses. This shows their trust and affection for the authors who compiled this book. The authors appreciate each of them and sincerely wish them continued success in life and fluent speech.

Are you a Person Who stammers / stutters?

Are you a parent of a PWS?

A sibling of a PWS?

A close friend of a PWS?

A teacher?

An employer?

An HR?

Then this book is for you.

We are sure that reading this book will significantly transform the lives of all who stammer.

The Authors

V. Manimaran

J. Agnee Raj

TAMIL SUPER SPEAKERS GROUP (TSS GROUP)

In most of the stories in this book, you will find references to "Tamil Super Speakers Group" or "TSS Group."

What is the Tamil Super Speakers Group?

I, Mr. Manimaran, created WhatsApp groups in 2014 to help people who stammer. In January 2014, a Tamil group was formed. Later that year, in August, an English group was created.

At first, these two groups were named "Tamil Stammering Group" and "Stammering Group (English)." However, a North Indian member suggested that *"stammering"* should not be in the group's name because everyone must aim to speak well. He proposed renaming the English group to "Super Speakers." This suggestion was accepted, and the English group was renamed the "Super Speakers" group.

Later, the Tamil group was also renamed "Tamil Super Speakers." Over the time, the following additional groups were launched:

* Malayalam Super Speakers Group – August 2020

* Telugu Super Speakers Group – November 2020

* Hindi Super Speakers Group – June 2021

Together, these five groups now have around 750 members.

Daily Activities of Group Members:

In these groups, members are expected to perform the following daily activities:

1. Daily Speech Practice Logging – Each member must report how long they practiced speech therapy each day, how many days they have completed it, and how many more days they plan to continue.

   Example:

   I, Ramesh, practiced speech from 6:00 AM to 7:00 AM today (30.03.2025) – 56/365." This means Ramesh practiced for 1 hour on March 30th and has completed 56 days out of his 365-day goal.

2. Voice Recording on a Daily Topic—A topic is given daily, and members must upload a voice recording of at least 3 minutes duration. Why 3 minutes? Many people who stammer believe they cannot speak fluently beyond a few words. Initially, they might hesitate even to record 1 minute, but within a few months, they start sending 3-minute recordings. Over time, with increased confidence, some members even send 30-minute recordings.

3. The group's Managing Director (Agnee Raj) listens to and reviews these recordings and provides feedback.

4. Q&A on Stammering – Members can ask questions about stammering in the group. All questions are answered within the same day.

5. Weekly Self-Help Meetings—The group shares details about the venue and time of weekly meetings, and interested members can attend.

6. Google Online Meetings – Details about these meetings are shared within the group.

7. Bi-Annual Workshops – Two workshops are conducted yearly, and announcements are made in the group.

8. Celebrating Achievements – If any member accomplishes something significant, their success is highlighted in the group to encourage and inspire others.

9. Posting Restrictions—Messages such as "Good Morning," birthday or wedding anniversary wishes, and festival greetings are strictly forbidden.

10. No Politics or Religion – Political, religious, or controversial posts are prohibited.

I initially managed the group until 2018. Within six months of joining, Mr. Agnee Raj began actively participating. Impressed by his enthusiasm, I appointed him as the Managing Director of the TSS group. Since then, Agnee Raj has been managing the Tamil group.

He made all the members post in Tamil instead of English. After becoming Managing Director, member participation not only significantly improved but also increased as more new members joined. He speaks with each new member and helps them gain a complete understanding of stammering.

I consider Agnee Raj a precious gem for the group. All members owe him a great appreciation for his role as Director.

– V. Manimaran

FOREWORD

Every person needs an example to accomplish something in life. Very few create a new path of their own. For many, it is easier to travel the path already laid out by someone.

No one had ever scored a double century in the 40-year history of One Day International (ODI) cricket. No one even imagined it was possible. In 2010, Sachin Tendulkar became the first player to score a double century in an ODI. The very next year, Virender Sehwag also scored a double century. Before that, no one believed it was even achievable.

Once one person did it, others began to believe they could do it, too. Today, many players have scored double-centuries. Given this trend, someone will likely score a double century in a T20 match someday.

Similarly, many people do not believe that stammerers can overcome their stammering or lead a successful life while still stammering. But that belief has been broken. Many stammerers have overcome their condition and continue to live successful and joyful lives like everyone else.

Here, we have compiled the success stories of 40 such individuals.

This book," *The Success Stories of People Who Stammer (PWS)*", highlights stammerers' challenges and how they fight them to succeed. It will serve as a motivational tool for stammerers and help them realise their dreams.

I extend my heartfelt thanks to everyone who contributed to the making of this book. Had the Tamil Super Speakers group been available to me before my marriage, I would have overcome my stammering much earlier. I can confidently say that my son would not have developed a stammer either.

This group aims to help individuals overcome stammering and benefit the next generation.

The primary reason behind compiling this book is to instil in every stammerer who reads it the firm belief that they, too, can live a successful life despite stammering and overcome the speech problem too to a great extent.

I hope every stammerer who reads this book will experience a powerful psychological transformation and a surge of confidence.

With best wishes,

J. Agnee Raj, Madurai

1
MADURAI TO SCOTLAND

FORTY YEARS AGO...

Thirty kilometres from Madurai city lies a village named Pandiyarajapuram, home to about a thousand people. Balasubramanian was born into a very simple family in this village.

It was only when he turned three that his parents began to realise that their child had great difficulty speaking. He stammered heavily, his words stumbling and halting mid-sentence.

Balu shares: In the village, I became entertainment for most people. Ten or more would sit around me, call me over, and ask me questions. As a little boy, I would be terrified. My heartbeat would rise. If I stammered while answering, they would laugh and enjoy it. It felt like torture. I would go home and cry alone. No one cared about my suffering.

He explains that stammering is 95% hereditary. His grandfather's relative had it, and so did his aunt. She's over 60 now, and the stammer seems to have passed from her to him.

Throughout primary and high school, Balu struggled immensely. He had no friends and wouldn't speak to anyone. After school, he would go home—he had no social life. People mocked him: "Who would even talk to this guy?"

Even if he knew the answer, he couldn't say it out loud in the classroom. The other students laughed and teased him, saying, "By the time you finish talking, class will be over!"

He studied for a Diploma in Mechanical Engineering at Nachi Muthu Polytechnic in Pollachi. Coming from a poor background, he received a ₹600 annual scholarship, which helped cover his mess fees. During the roll call, his number was 678. When the lecturer reached that number, the entire class burst out laughing. He couldn't say "Present, Sir" correctly or quickly, so he would just sit silently, and the lecturer would mark him present. His stammering was a source of constant ridicule.

DESPERATE ATTEMPTS TO OVERCOME STAMMERING

You might ask—did he try to fix it? The answer: Yes, obsessively.

He tried every method available, even more than what most in Tamil Nadu might have tried. He experimented relentlessly as if possessed.

* He practiced speaking with small pebbles in his mouth for several months.

* A homoeopathy doctor near Pollachi suggested rubbing rock salt on his tongue to reduce its thickness. He did this between 1980 and 1982. It was a painful and arduous experience.

* He underwent two full treatments with a Siddha doctor in Thiruvidaimarudur.

* Tried hypnotherapy with Dr. R.M. Somasundaram.

* Underwent acupuncture at T. Kallupatti near Madurai. Thirty to forty needles were pricked into his body with low-voltage electric currents. It lasted two weeks—with no result.

✳ He stood in a well, neck-deep in water, and practiced speaking early in the morning when no one was around. He had read about it somewhere. Again—there are no results.

During polytechnic studies, one must attach a revenue stamp to a receipt to collect scholarship money. He couldn't pronounce "revenue stamp," so he asked in Tamil for a "stamp to stick for receiving money." The post office staff assumed he didn't know English and mocked him harshly.

You're in a polytechnic and don't even know what a 'revenue stamp' is? Are you on scholarship, too? If everyone were like you, how would the country improve? It felt like being hit with a hammer. That humiliation only fueled my determination to get cured.

STRUGGLES WITH EMPLOYMENT

I scored well in my final Polytechnic exams and passed successfully. I applied for jobs and received interview calls from a few places. I went to Chennai twice. Although I knew the correct answers to the interview questions, I couldn't speak them out. A kind of fear took over. I was unable to speak. Even for simple questions, I couldn't respond, and they would look at me mockingly, thinking, *"Why is he like this?"* I didn't get the job.

My uncle worked at a company called 'Madhura Sugars.' Through his recommendation, I got a job there without attending an interview. While working in shifts, I found it challenging to interact with many people. I felt that my speech difficulty should not affect the company's work. So, I requested a transfer to the Drawing Section (the department that prepares engineering drawings), where I wouldn't have to talk much with others. The office work continued without any issues. However, the intense desire to overcome my speech problem remained strong within me. I continued trying various methods.

TURNING POINT – 1986

A major turning point in my life occurred in 1986 with an event. That year, I read an article in a magazine that said stammering could be completely cured. I felt an incredible thrill—an intense excitement for the first time. Wanting to know more about the treatment, I wrote a personal letter to the editor of that magazine. I received a reply very quickly. He wrote, "That article was from the BBC. If you contact them, you can get more details." So, I wrote a letter to the BBC in London.

Andrew Bell, a 58-year-old civil engineer from Scotland, had suffered from stammering. His mother was a great support and encouragement to him. Through his efforts, Andrew Bell was able to cure himself of his stammering. I wrote to him about myself and my speech difficulties, requesting his help.

I received a reply. Andrew wrote that no appointments were available for treatment for the next one and a half years (20 months) as it was already fully booked. He advised that it would be best to register in December 1986. I wrote back confirming that I would come. Do you know how hard it was for me to travel abroad?

At that time, I had just spent nearly one lakh rupees on my sister's wedding, so I didn't have the money to go abroad. The maximum I could manage was ₹15,000. I received ₹25,000 as help from my future father-in-law. A few friends also helped me.

Obtaining approval from the Reserve Bank was complicated. I had to submit a certificate from a government doctor stating that "there is no proper treatment for this condition in India, and it cannot be cured here."

When I went to the Chennai Government General Hospital to request a certificate, they said, "Get treated here itself." Under the supervision of an assistant, I had to read a book aloud continuously. The treatment lasted two weeks. But I didn't feel any confidence. Moreover, they admitted that a complete cure would be difficult. They said they would "consider" issuing a certificate only after six months of treatment. Even then, they didn't guarantee that they would issue it.

This was during my time working at Madhura Sugars. Through office contacts, I approached an IAS officer and explained my situation. He was a kind-hearted person who spoke directly with the hospital's Dean. As a result, I received the required medical certificate.

Once all the formalities were completed, I was ready to go to London. Before that, I had never even seen the inside of an aeroplane. I hadn't even travelled first class on a train.

I landed at London Heathrow Airport. After asking several people for directions, I took the underground train to the BBC office.

A woman at the reception noticed that I was speaking with a stammer. She patiently told me the names of several staff members individually and helped me meet Anandhi. With Anandhi's assistance, I reached the city of Edinburgh.

From Edinburgh, I travelled to Kirkcaldy, about 40 kilometres away, where Andrew's class began in August 1988.

The program lasted only six days. Andrew did not give us any medicine, pills, or injections.

Apart from a single handshake, he didn't even touch us. There was no hypnosis involved, and he didn't use any electrical devices.

Kirkcaldy, Andrew's hometown, had a population of 55,000. He arranged for our stay at a hotel in the area. The total cost of the course and accommodation came to ₹20,000. The round-trip airfare was ₹10,500.

There were seventeen of us in total. Participants came from England, Sri Lanka, Belgium, Holland, and Pakistan—14 men and three women. I was the only one from India.

In the announcement for his treatment, Andrew had mentioned that the fee was £400, and if the treatment didn't work for anyone, he would refund their course fee, travel expenses, and hotel charges.

The core idea of Andrew's treatment was: *"One must build self-confidence in the subconscious mind. The thought and fear that 'I cannot speak' will automatically vanish."* That was the essence and subtlety of his method.

Andrew asked each of us simple questions, such as, "Who are you? How did you get *here?"* and recorded our responses on a video camera. Every day, he taught us a few exercises. He explained how to breathe correctly and how to pronounce words.

He trained us to start by speaking simple words. Once back in the hotel room, he instructed us to practice individually for fifteen minutes.

Andrew implemented three techniques: physical exercises, practicing as if speaking on stage, and group conversations.

Every day, I noticed a 15% improvement. I couldn't believe it. Within six days, I was speaking clearly.

It was a pure thrill! I have always been afraid of the telephone. I used to wonder whether I'd ever be able to speak on the phone one day. But I was talking on the phone with Aanandhi Suryaprakash in London. Halfway through the conversation, I broke down in tears—tears of joy.

I gave an interview to a local newspaper in Scotland as the only Indian who had come from India, undergone the treatment, and been completely cured. I spoke about my struggles and how I managed to get there. It was the first interview I had ever given, and it was published in the September 20, 1988 edition of that newspaper.

Sankaramurthy of BBC Tamil also interviewed me. The interview lasted seven minutes and was broadcast on September 22, 1988. My voice would have been heard all around the world that day. I couldn't believe it myself!

They gave me thirty-five pounds—nearly a thousand rupees—as an honorarium. This was money I earned through speaking.

While returning to India from London on a Sabena Airlines flight, many thoughts crossed my mind: "I have eliminated a major flaw in myself." *This is a considerable achievement. From now on, I can achieve anything in life. Why shouldn't I share this with others?"* That was when I decided, right there during the flight, to teach this to other stammerers as well.

PAYING IT FORWARD

I married my close relative, Valarmathi, on November 6, 1988. (Before going to London, I had seen three prospective brides. Though the families were okay with me, the accompanying relatives rejected me because I had a stammer. That's another story.)

I continued working at Madhura Sugars. Driven by a strong passion to help others overcome their stammering, I took action.

I rented rooms in a large lodge in Madurai and conducted six-day courses. I advertised in the daily newspapers of Madurai. I used my annual leave granted by the company each year to conduct these courses. I received an excellent response.

So far, around 850 people have attended the courses I conducted. Of them, 750 people have been cured, with a success rate of 90% to 100%. The remaining 100 had only partial improvement due to a lack of interest and effort on their part.

In six cases where women's marriages had been stalled because of stammering, those obstacles were overcome, and the women are now happily married and well-settled in life.

Many participants from the same family—such as fathers and daughters, brothers, and sisters—attended the course together and have been completely cured.

Six young men completed their engineering degrees and went to the United States, where they now work as college professors and engineers. Fifteen others are employed in the Gulf countries.

People aged 18 to 60 have attended the training. All I expect from them is their full cooperation.

The hardships I faced until the age of 24 while living with my speech disorder are indescribable.

However, after visiting Scotland, receiving speech training, and overcoming my stammering, my self-confidence soared many times. I developed a mindset that allowed me to succeed in any profession I chose.

FROM SPEECH STRUGGLES TO BUSINESS SUCCESS

I resigned from my government job and started a new foundry business with the help of friends I met through the course. Today, I run three factories with over 100 employees, manufacturing iron spare parts and generating a turnover in crores of Rupees. We export casting spare parts to countries like Dubai, Malaysia, Germany, and the United States.

I have travelled to Singapore, Malaysia, Cambodia, Indonesia, England, Belgium, Italy, Switzerland, China, Australia, and Vietnam.

Attending an interview used to be a struggle for me. But today, I am a respected person in society and an inspiration to others. All of this is thanks to the treatment I received in Scotland.

I've already mentioned my marriage—my wife is a relative and a homemaker. I have two sons; both are engineers, and both are married. Each of them has a daughter. My two sons are now managing the foundry business.

My life is now moving forward with happiness and peace.

Believe in yourself. The sky is within your reach.

S. Balasubramanian – Coimbatore - Tamil Nadu

Email: modernfoundry@yahoo.com

2

LIGHTHOUSE

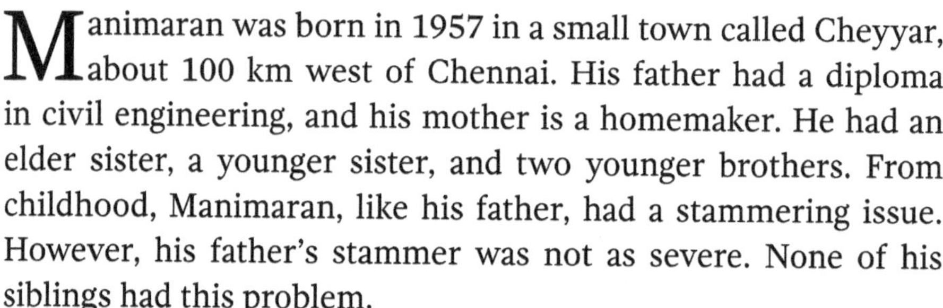

Manimaran was born in 1957 in a small town called Cheyyar, about 100 km west of Chennai. His father had a diploma in civil engineering, and his mother is a homemaker. He had an elder sister, a younger sister, and two younger brothers. From childhood, Manimaran, like his father, had a stammering issue. However, his father's stammer was not as severe. None of his siblings had this problem.

During his school days, when attendance was taken, his classmates would respond with "Present Sir," but Manimaran would say "Yes Sir" instead, as pronouncing "Present Sir" was very difficult for him.

Despite this, his classmates never mocked or teased him because he was a bright student and consistently ranked first. Though he won many prizes in handwriting and essay competitions, he was disappointed that he couldn't participate in quizzes or speech contests due to his speech difficulty.

In the 11th standard board exams in 1973, Manimaran scored 100 out of 100 in mathematics, just like his father. However, he held his father's achievement in higher regard because his father studied under far more difficult conditions without even access to electricity. In contrast, Manimaran had many conveniences, including guidance from his father and a tuition master, to help him succeed.

He studied Civil Engineering at the Regional Engineering College (REC) in Tiruchirappalli from 1974 to 1979. His father had completed his civil engineering diploma (LCE) between 1949 and 1952. His father proudly used to say, "I studied at Guindy Engineering College," because back then, even diploma courses were taught there. Later, the Central Polytechnic College (CPT) was newly built in Adyar, and diploma courses were moved there. Incidentally, Manimaran's father was part of the last batch that studied at Guindy. Even in college, during roll call, Manimaran would respond with his usual "Yes, Sir."

His college classmates came from well-educated families and didn't look down on his stammer. They didn't tease him; even the professors and lecturers were supportive. However, one sad aspect was that although Manimaran often knew the answers, he would not respond to questions or ask doubts during class because of his speech problem.

During holidays, he would go to Tiruchirappalli town with his close friends Jaganathan and Bindu. They helped him order food at restaurants, do shopping, and buy bus and movie tickets. He usually avoided going out alone. He carried the exact change for bus tickets if he had no choice. When he didn't have a change, he would tell the conductor the fare instead of the destination name, as that was easier for him. Sometimes, instead of naming his actual destination, which he found hard to pronounce, he would mention a farther location with an easier name to avoid stammering.

1979, after completing college, he registered at the employment exchange in Chennai. At that time, the state government was one of the major employers of civil engineers. Luckily, during that period, the Tamil Nadu government had many job openings for civil engineers. There were no written or interview exams—only certificates were verified. The Chennai Metrowater Supply Board selected Manimaran. However, once he joined, his fear and anxiety over his stammering increased significantly.

As mentioned earlier, after entering the job, his speech disorder caused great distress because his role involved frequent interaction with the public and senior officials. His heartbeat would increase whenever he had to face the public, and he'd feel jittery. His breathing would become irregular, and he would stammer heavily. The same happened when speaking to higher officials or in public settings. Still, because of his dedication and integrity at work, his senior officers overlooked his speech difficulty and treated him kindly and naturally.

Due to his stammer, Manimaran faced many humiliating experiences. Two incidents stand out:

In one instance, a relative was admitted to a reputed hospital in Chennai. Since mobile phones were uncommon, he had to go to the hospital's reception counter to find the room number. The place was crowded. Anxiety and fear gripped him. No word came out when he tried to say the relative's name at the reception. The receptionist saw him struggle and laughed continuously for a full minute. People around looked at him strangely. He had never been so humiliated in his life. Somehow, he finally said the name with great difficulty and visited his relative's room. That incident haunted him for a whole week.

The second incident occurred when Manimaran had gone to Delhi for work. A friend of his was employed at an office there. Since it was a time before mobile phones, the friend gave Manimaran the landline number of his superior. When Manimaran dialled the number, the superior answered the call. Manimaran began stammering badly as he tried to say his friend's name. When the superior asked, "Whom do you want to speak to?" he continued to stammer while trying to say the name.

The superior asked who he was, and Manimaran struggled to say his name, designation, and friend's name while stammering.

The superior began ridiculing him: "How did you reach such a senior position?" "You can't even pronounce your name properly. How do you manage your office responsibilities?" "Which college gave you an engineering degree?" After these scathing remarks, the superior hung up the phone.

Manimaran couldn't even meet his friend. More than the pain of not seeing his friend, the humiliation of that call hurt him deeply.

He believes that every person who stammers must have experienced similar humiliations. Such moments hurt mentally and severely damage one's self-respect.

He feared hearing the telephone ring because he couldn't pronounce his name fluently. At the office, he would ask his assistant to answer the phone. If he had to talk to someone, he would ask the assistant to first call that person, and once the call was connected, Manimaran would only speak then.

Manimaran got married in 1983. Neither he nor his father informed the bride's family about his speech issue. Even now, he is unsure whether hiding it was right or wrong at the time. After marriage, his wife eventually asked him about his stammer. But she didn't take it as a big issue. Instead, she advised him to try to overcome it and encouraged him to speak slowly.

Even after 41 years of married life, Manimaran continues to be grateful to his wife. Not once has she shown disappointment due to his stammer. She has always supported him—ordering food at restaurants, buying bus and train tickets, and shopping. She accompanied him to three National Conferences (NC) of the Indian Stammering Association (TISA): the first two were held in Bhubaneswar and Kurukshetra, and the eighth one in Bengaluru. He sees his wife as an angel sent by God. He also expresses his gratitude to her father, mother, and two brothers, who never made an issue of his stammer.

People may ask if he ever sought treatment for his stammer. He did, but not in the same way as Mr. Balu (a notable figure in speech therapy). Here are some of the attempts he made:

Although his father also had a stammer, he managed life successfully. So Manimaran believes his father didn't give too much importance to his son's speech problem. Moreover, during those times, there were few speech therapists and no modern communication tools like the Internet to research the issue in depth.

Only after entering college did Manimaran realise the importance of speaking fluently. He went to the General Hospital (G.H.) in Chennai. In the 1970s, this hospital was considered the go-to place to treat all ailments. At that time, speciality hospitals with expert teams for each disorder didn't exist in Chennai.

At G.H., he was referred to a speech therapist—a term Manimaran heard for the first time. When he went to see the therapist, the person instructed about 10 children on pronouncing certain words. Manimaran explained his condition to the therapist. He was then asked to join the children for practice, which shocked him. He was 18 then, while the children were around 7 to 10.

Having no other choice, he joined them. The therapist instructed him to open his mouth wide and pronounce each word loudly and slowly. Manimaran followed those instructions for an hour.

He visited the therapist ten times a month and practiced as advised. But as he saw no improvement, he stopped going after a month.

A friend of Manimaran's later recommended that he consult a psychologist. Manimaran knew of one in Chennai. However, his stammer made him afraid to meet the doctor in person, so he wrote a letter (as there were no modern communication tools back then) explaining his stammering issue and requesting help.

Ten days later, the doctor replied, asking him to visit in person. Manimaran went and explained his issue. The psychologist prescribed two types of tablets and instructed him to take them daily without fail. The doctor assured the tablets would calm his mind and help him speak fluently.

After taking the tablets for the first three days, Manimaran noticed no change. On the fourth day, he began speaking with slightly less stammering. He felt immense joy and hope that he might finally speak fluently. However, this was only a short-lived improvement.

After a week of taking the medication, he began experiencing drowsiness and a kind of mental dullness most of the time. As a result, his productivity and work efficiency dropped, and he couldn't concentrate properly on any task. Manimaran consulted his family doctor about this. The doctor explained that stammering is a psychological issue and cannot be cured with pills. On the contrary, such medication would only cause side effects. Based on that advice, Manimaran immediately stopped taking the tablets.

As another attempt, he approached a speech therapist in T. Nagar, Chennai. After visiting the place, he realised it was a "Counseling Center" run by a few psychologists. Manimaran explained his speech issue to them. One gave him a newspaper and asked him to read it slowly using the *prolongation technique* for 30 minutes. Then, he was asked to converse slowly with the counsellor. For the next 30 minutes, Manimaran could speak fluently without interruptions. A spark of belief grew in him for the first time—that he could speak well.

He attended five sessions at the counselling centre. He understood that the prolongation technique allowed him to speak without stammering. However, he couldn't apply the same technique in public settings.

On the day of his fifth session, he went to a nearby tea stall to have some tea. But when he tried to say "tea," his voice got stuck, and nothing came out. He felt disappointed. He became frustrated with himself—unable to say even a simple one-syllable word like "tea." He realised that the prolongation method only worked in controlled environments like the centre but was ineffective in real-world situations, so he stopped going there.

Until the year 2000, Manimaran tried various ways to cure his stammer.

Eventually, he saw a ray of hope at the end of a dark tunnel. Yes! He went to his usual salon on a Sunday morning (January 21, 2001). Seeing the crowd there, he figured his turn would take at least half an hour. He picked up a supplementary book with the Dinamalar Tamil daily to pass the time.

There, he saw an article titled "Stammering? Not a Problem Anymore." The title immediately grabbed his attention. Having stammered since birth, he eagerly began reading the article.

It was a real-life story about an engineer who suffered from stammering and successfully overcame it.

The article, published in *Dinamalar's* supplement, was in two parts (dated January 21 and January 28, 2001). Manimaran found the story both inspiring and motivating. It was the success story of Mr. Balasubramaniam, which you've already read in the first chapter of this book.

After reading Mr. Balu's article, Manimaran wrote him a letter. Mr. Balu promptly replied, asking him to meet in person the next time he visited Chennai.

One day, in a Chennai lodge, Manimaran met Mr. Balu. After asking a few questions, Balu expressed concern about whether

Manimaran, at his age, would be able to follow the training with full commitment (Manimaran was 42 years old at the time). Manimaran assured him that he would diligently follow all the techniques and instructions. Mr. Balu agreed, albeit with some hesitation, to admit him into the training program.

Balu said the training would be conducted over six days in Madurai. During those days, everyone must stay at a designated lodge and not go out. He also instructed them not to make any phone calls.

Manimaran reached Madurai a day before the training began. He was given a shared room at a lodge. His roommate was Surendran, a civil engineer from Madurai who also stammered like Manimaran.

On the night before the training, Mr. Balu visited the lodge and informed everyone that the training would start at 9 a.m. sharp and that they should be ready. He also advised them to eat only a light breakfast the following day.

The training began the next morning at nine sharp. Twenty people with stammering participated. Mr. Balu called each of them forward and asked them to speak for a few minutes. All of this was recorded on video. Then, he began the training.

He first instructed them to do some physical exercises. After that, he taught everyone speech exercises. Following an hour of speech training, Mr. Balu divided the group into 10 pairs. He then asked each pair to engage in slow, fluent conversation for 15 minutes.

He was asked to continue the speech practice for another hour, which he did along with the others. After that, everyone was given a book and told to read it slowly for 15 minutes. All of these activities together formed a cycle.

For five consecutive days, all participants followed three such cycles. Mr. Balu allowed a 15-minute break in the morning and evening for tea and a 30-minute break for lunch. For lunch, light meals like tomato rice or lemon rice were provided.

Each day, the training ended at 6 PM. Mr. Balu instructed everyone to speak slowly, even during informal interactions. He had even trained the lodge staff to speak in the same slow manner. He emphasised that everyone must follow the slow speech technique from when they woke up until the training began at 9 AM the next morning. This approach was used to gradually break their habit of fast speech and replace it with a slower speech pattern.

Thus, the training continued for five days. This habit of slow speech began replacing their old, fast speech style. By the end of the fifth day, everyone was speaking fluently without stammering. They were excited by the improvement in their speech and gained a new hope that they could now live a life free from stammering.

On the sixth morning, Mr. Balu arranged a telephone conversation practice. Everyone was able to speak fluently over the phone. Later, Mr. Balu had each person speak again, just like on the first day and recorded them on video.

He then showed both videos—the one from the first day and the one after training—on a TV to highlight the improvements in their speech due to the training. After watching and comparing both videos, the participants were filled with joy upon seeing their progress.

All 20 participants stammered when they began the training. However, after five days of consistent speech practice, they could all speak fluently.

Mr. Balu warned them that unless they continued speech practice for at least one hour every morning, it would be challenging to maintain the improvements or fully overcome stammering.

Five others from Chennai who had trained alongside Manimaran were among the participants. He suggested they meet once a week in a public place in Chennai to encourage and track each other's progress. Everyone agreed.

They decided to meet on Sundays near the Gandhi statue at Marina Beach. In the meantime, Manimaran began practicing his speech every morning for one hour. The six of them met every week at Marina Beach and shared the progress they had made in their speech.

For the next six months, everything went smoothly as planned. Manimaran could speak fluently for 15 minutes continuously at the training centre in his office. Everyone praised the improvement in his speech.

At 43, Manimaran realised he could speak fluently without stammering for the first time. That joy gave him the feeling that he was standing at the top of the world.

However, after six months, one day, his health deteriorated suddenly, and he couldn't continue his speech practice. As a result, he began stammering again, which caused him deep emotional distress.

A month later, after recovering, he went to Marina Beach on a Sunday. But none of the other five people showed up.

Meanwhile, Manimaran received a promotion to Executive Cadre at his office, which changed the nature of his work. He now had to work day and sometimes night, also without regular breaks.

Due to this hectic work schedule, he could no longer find time for morning speech practice. During these early hours, the maximum benefit from speech training is achieved.

Still, due to the six months of consistent training he had previously completed, he could speak reasonably well, with minimal stammering. He was also able to speak well during office meetings for short durations. Compared to before 2001, he had started leading a significantly better life.

That was before mobile phones, WhatsApp, or Facebook. Without modern communication tools, Manimaran could not stay in touch with other stammering people, so the weekly meetings stopped. Unlike in Western countries, India had no "support groups" for people who stammer. As a result, Manimaran eventually discontinued his speech practice.

He realised that it is extremely difficult for a person to continue speech practice independently without a support group. However, he now firmly believed that if he continued practicing speech regularly, he could speak as well as anyone else.

In 2009, a new turning point came into his life: TISA (The Indian Stammering Association). Yes—at 52, this became the most significant breakthrough in his life.

Before learning about TISA, Manimaran used to resent his stammering deeply. He never spoke openly about it with anyone. The fear and shame stayed bottled up inside him. Every time he had to say in public, the pressure of stammering put him under chronic mental stress.

"Acceptance of stammering" is the core philosophy of TISA (The Indian Stammering Association). Rather than constantly worrying about stammering, one must accept it and speak openly about it with others. This helps reduce the fear and shame of stammering, allowing people to gradually speak more fluently.

Dr. Satyendra Srivastava (fondly called Dr. Sachin) is the founder of TISA. Under his guidance, Manimaran was appointed the Coordinator for the TISA Chennai Chapter. The inaugural event was formally conducted in 2009 at the YWCA International Guest House in Egmore, Chennai.

At the event, Dr. B.K. Singh gave a speech and shared two experiences from his life. Manimaran recounts these here because they reveal how devastating stammering can be in certain situations.

Before sharing those incidents, here are a few words about Dr. B.K. Singh: He was also a stammerer. He earned a degree and later a doctorate in psychology. Through his efforts, he overcame stammering and in 2000 started the Suraj Stammering Care Centre in Maihar, a town in Satna district, Madhya Pradesh.

The first incident Dr. Singh shared was that after completing his psychology degree, he was searching for a job and had to attend an interview. He had to travel by train and reached the station just a few minutes before the train's arrival. He stood in line to buy a ticket, but when it was his turn, he couldn't say the name of the destination due to his stammer. With the train approaching, people behind him pushed him aside, bought their tickets, and left. The train arrived and departed while Dr. Singh stood silently, unable to speak. As a result, he missed the interview entirely.

The second incident was even more traumatic. While working at a factory job unrelated to his academic field, Dr. Singh had a night shift. He and another worker were operating machinery when the other person accidentally got his hand stuck in a moving machine. Blood started gushing out. The only way to call an ambulance was via an intercom, but Dr. Singh couldn't speak—his throat choked, and not a word came out. He began to panic and even started to faint. Luckily, another employee entered the area, understood the urgency, and called the ambulance using the intercom.

Even as he recounted this incident, Dr. Singh said his hands and legs trembled. Incidents like these are a harsh reality for many people who stammer. In such moments, one might even question the value of life itself.

After the Chennai Chapter was started, Manimaran promoted the meetings in various ways and conducted weekly gatherings at YWCA. He invited many experts, teachers, and school students to attend and participate.

Even in his official duties, Manimaran never slacked. In South India, for the first time, he played a key role in setting up a wastewater treatment plant that used the methane gas generated during treatment to power a gas engine that produced electricity. The electricity generated was sufficient to run the entire treatment plant, resulting in lakhs of rupees in savings on the electricity bill. Manimaran was a key contributor to the project's success from beginning to end. He later went to Chennai Metro Rail Limited (CMRL) on deputation and worked for five years. Due to his hard work at CMRL, he received an 'Outstanding' performance rating for five consecutive years, and in 2012, he was promoted to Chief Engineer. In 2013, for personal reasons, he opted for voluntary retirement.

After retirement in 2013, he attended the 3rd TISA National Conference, held in Delhi from October 3 to 5, and was elected as the TISA National Coordinator.

Meanwhile, on December 9, 2013, he launched the Chennai Stammering Care Center (CSCC) in Kottur, Chennai. He vacated a rental unit in his apartment complex and used that space to start the CSCC. With ample time after retirement, Manimaran resumed daily speech practice.

He firmly believes that most people who stammer are willing to do speech practice to overcome it. However, a significant obstacle is the lack of a consistent support group to motivate daily practice.

To address this, he created a WhatsApp group on January 1, 2014, to send daily motivational messages to people who stammer. Today, there are about five WhatsApp groups with around 500 members, organised by language:

1. Tamil

2. English

3. Hindi

4. Malayalam

5. Telugu

However, due to severe joint pain and difficulty walking, Manimaran's ability to travel was significantly reduced. As a result, in June 2014, he requested to step down from his role as TISA National Coordinator. Understanding his condition, the TISA management accepted his request and relieved him from his duties.

Through CSCC (Chennai Stammering Care Centre), Manimaran continued his service by offering speech practice and guidance to those seeking to overcome stammering.

But fate had other plans. Due to persistent headaches and a balance problem, his health began to deteriorate, eventually reaching a point where even walking normally became a challenge.

Despite these physical difficulties, he continued visiting CSCC in Kottur once a week. Over time, however, it became increasingly complex for him to walk, and with a heavy heart and no other option, he was forced to close CSCC. This was one of the saddest events of his life. Because of his health, he had to stop speech practice for a second time.

Even after consulting six top neurologists in Chennai, his condition did not improve. He appointed Vinoth Kumar, another group member, as admin and exited the WhatsApp group. For the next two years, apart from doctor visits, he remained confined to his home. It was a painful phase in his life.

Manimaran then posted a detailed message about his health condition on a Yahoo Group by his college classmates. One of his friends, S.N. Srikanth, read it and called him. He recommended a neuropsychiatrist, who also happened to be a close family friend. Trusting Srikanth and having no other option, Manimaran consulted the specialist.

The doctor conducted detailed evaluations and tests, finally diagnosing Autonomic Dysfunction. He explained that while it may not be fully curable, it could be managed and improved through physiotherapy, acupuncture, Ayurveda, and counselling.

Manimaran began these treatments immediately. After six months, despite much improvement, he continued with faith and persistence, as he had no alternatives.

From May 2017, his condition gradually started improving. He was able to concentrate better and began re-engaging with the WhatsApp groups. With renewed energy, he started serving the stammering community again. However, he permanently stopped speech practice because of a nerve issue in his neck— every time he tried to practice, he developed a severe headache within minutes.

Still, his social service continued. He offered every bit of advice possible to those who reached out to him. His service continues today, and his health is much better.

Manimaran deeply understands that only a person who stammers can truly understand the daily struggles of another person who stammers. He also knows that many stammerers are reluctant to talk about it—even with their parents, siblings, friends, or fellow stammerers.

He now offers counselling at his home to those seeking help for stammering. He uses WhatsApp to share exercises, engage people in regular activities, and boost their self-confidence. Notably, he offers all these services completely free of charge.

He is aware that stammering awareness is very low in India. Unlike Western countries, India lacks sufficient support groups and speech therapists, a significant gap.

Even books about stammering are written mainly by authors from abroad. Few Indian authors have written on the subject, and most books don't include simple, practical, home-based exercises.

So, Manimaran wrote a book, initially in English, drawing on his experience with over 700 people who stammer and the knowledge he gained from TISA. He published his English book in 2019.

Later that same year, he translated it into Tamil and published it. In 2021, Hemant Kumar, a fellow stammerer, translated it into Hindi. In 2024, Prakash, a Malayalam-speaking member, translated it into Malayalam. Both these individuals did the translations without accepting any payment or honorarium. Manimaran expresses his heartfelt gratitude to both of them.

So far, over 2,200 copies of the book (across all four languages) have been sold.

The speech exercises mentioned in the book are very simple and designed to be practiced daily. Many are eager to know how long it takes to overcome stammering. But rather than expecting an instant solution or *band-aid fix*, Manimaran stresses that consistent and structured practice is essential.

Stammering is not something that can be cured overnight. First, one must understand the whole picture—what stammering is, what it isn't, and how to change one's mindset and approach. That's the only way to find a lasting solution.

It's easier said than done. There is no automatic device that can "fix" it. One must build a strong foundation with long-term planning and discipline to maintain results.

The time it takes to overcome stammering varies based on several factors:

* Age

* Severity of the issue

* Dedication to practice

* Application of techniques in daily life

Finally, readers might wonder: How does Manimaran speak today?

He has recovered about 95% from stammering. Due to the medical reasons mentioned earlier, he had to permanently stop speech practice so that he couldn't achieve 100% fluency.

However, he has wholly overcome fear and shame, which allows him to speak confidently in all situations. If someone asks about his current speech condition, he boldly replies:

"Yes, I still stammer."

If he were to say, "I'm completely cured," he believes he'd start stammering again immediately! But if he says, "I might stammer, and I'm okay with it," he'll speak fluently.

That's the strange nature of stammering. That's the psychology behind it. Once this subtle truth is understood, it's like crossing half the well.

Anyone who follows the techniques outlined in Manimaran's book with patience and conviction will never again wonder, *"Can stammering be cured?"*

One key message from his book:

"Being born with stammering is not your fault. But dying with it, is."

So, Manimaran wishes that every person who stammers should:

- ✲ Work hard
- ✲ Accept their condition wholeheartedly
- ✲ Practice speech exercises
- ✲ Make progress in communication
- ✲ Eliminate fear completely
- ✲ And lead a fulfilling life.

He welcomes anyone to contact him via WhatsApp at +91 98842 89989

V. Manimaran – Chennai - Tamil Nadu

Email: manimaran1957@yahoo.com & manimaran57@gmail.com

3

GLOWING LAMP

His name is J. Agnee Raj (age 42). He was born in 1983 as the second child in a farming family with three children in the village of Chettikulam (Umachikulam) in the northern part of Madurai district. He has an elder sister and a younger brother.

Like everyone else, his childhood began with joy. When he was in the third grade, his uncle, who lived on the next street, brought over a drawing of a peacock made by his cousin. Agnee Raj excitedly showed it to everyone in his house. At that moment, his uncle told his father, "Even if your sons carry milk offerings to Lord Palani for 18 years, they won't be able to draw like my son." Whether his uncle said it seriously or jokingly is unknown, but it deeply affected Agnee Raj. From that day on, he started practicing drawing peacocks and other art.

Once, when he was in the fifth grade, his teacher asked a question. When Agnee Raj stood up to answer, his tongue twisted, his lips trembled, and words refused to come out. He thought, *what is this? I know the answer well: why isn't it coming out?* The teacher caned him before he could process it, and his mind went blank. More than the boys laughing, the girls' laughter brought him great shame.

But could he leave it at that?

After all, he was a Madurai native!

Would he give up so easily?

Unable to bear the embarrassment, he immediately wrote the answer on the slate and showed it, using that as a temporary balm for his shame.

That was the moment Agnee Raj realised that he was not speaking normally. It was from that incident that he understood he was a person who stammers.

However, he didn't let go of his passion for art. In the eighth grade, he participated in a district-level drawing competition and won second prize. The art teacher praised him at the school assembly, saying, "If anyone can draw better than me in this school, it is only Agnee Raj." From then on, his focus was entirely on becoming an art teacher.

That same year, his school hosted district-level talent competitions. Agnee Raj participated in the singing category and won first prize at the district level, bringing honour to his school.

A few days after that event, the teacher asked a question during a science class. When Agnee Raj tried to answer, his stammer delayed his response. The teacher, thinking he was pretending not to know the answer, shouted, *"How come you don't stammer when singing? You won first prize at the district level in singing! But when I ask a question, suddenly you stammer? Who are you trying to fool? If you don't know the answer, say so. Don't pretend to stammer!"*

Then he hit him.

That day, the humiliation hurt more than the beating. He didn't have the heart to share this with anyone at home. Like many such incidents, he buried it deep within.

Still, Agnee Raj felt the teacher's words were justified.

"Why don't I stammer while singing? It's the same mouth singing—why can't it speak properly?"

This question grew big inside him, and he didn't yet know the answer.

Somehow, he completed his eighth-grade exams and went to his maternal uncle's village near Vathalakundu for vacation. He didn't know then that a great thunderbolt was about to strike both his happiness and his dreams.

Two weeks before school was set to reopen, his father passed away. All of Agnee Raj's dreams were cremated along with his father's ashes.

Agnee Raj's father left the world, placing the burden of all responsibilities on his young shoulders—an illiterate mother, a sister nearing marriageable age, and a younger brother still in school with a future ahead.

Until then, Agnee Raj had a mild stammer, but after his father's death, anxiety about the future gripped him, and his stammering worsened. His interest in studies began to decline.

Agnee Raj, who had consistently ranked in the top five until 8th grade, couldn't believe he passed the 10th-grade exams. That shows how far his academics had slipped. He barely passed 10th grade, like a blind cat stumbling upon a mouse.

At that point, he thought about finding a job to reduce his mother's burden. However, his relatives insisted that he pursue vocational training for two years. From 1999 to 2001, he completed it. But when he began searching for a job, Agnee Raj faced many rejections due to his stammering.

He eventually found a job and learned the trade by God's grace. Until then, his mother had worked as a farm labourer. Agnee Raj asked her to stop working, promising to take full responsibility for the family. He encouraged her to take a rest and willingly took on the burden alone.

In 2002, his sister's wedding took place. At just 18 years of age, Agnee Raj incurred a debt of ₹1.5 lakhs.

In 2004, when he was 20 years old, he asked his family for money to start a business. But how could the family have any savings? He was the only one earning. So, he pleaded with his relatives to help him borrow money. But they questioned, "You can't even speak properly—how will you run a business?"

There was already wedding debt. And now more loans? "Forget all that; just stick to your job," they said. Because of his stammering, he began to feel disabled and unworthy. But Madurai natives are known for their determination and fighting spirit! Would he give up so easily? He had a burning desire: *"I will rise in the very place I was humiliated."*

He cried silently, stopped eating, and isolated himself from everyone. Seeing his resolve, someone finally lent him the ₹25,000 he had requested.

On February 11, 2004, he started a shop, JPN SPARES & TOOLS, selling electrical spare parts. With every past humiliation and scar fresh in his memory, Agnee Raj focused entirely on growing the business. Within just two years of starting the shop, he paid off all his debts and rose to a position where he could financially help the people who once lent him money.

Due to circumstances, he couldn't continue his education, but he made sure his younger brother studied the course of his choice: Diploma in Electrical and Electronics Engineering (EEE).

He took up all responsibilities for his mother and brother so that his mother would never feel the absence of a husband and the children would not feel fatherless. He performed every duty with care and pride.

After completing those duties, in 2010, the talk of Agnee Raj's marriage began.

He often wondered, *"Who would marry someone like me who stammers?"*

As expected, one prospective bride's family rejected him due to his stammering.

He sarcastically praised himself, saying, *"My prediction never fails!"*

He later understood that it wasn't just the rejection that stung—it was the fact that his family had hidden his stammering from the bride's side, and once they found out, they rejected him.

Even though Agnee Raj told his family to be upfront with the bride's side and mentioned that the groom had a stammer, his family disagreed. However, since he couldn't handle another rejection, he met the next prospective bride and openly shared about his speech problem.

Surprisingly, the bride's family didn't make a big issue. They understood that what mattered most was that Agnee Raj was doing well in his business, earning a steady income, responsibly caring for a fatherless family, and living a disciplined life. They believed employment and good character defined a man—not speech fluency. That's when Agnee Raj realised that stammering was not necessarily a barrier to marriage.

He married and had two children—the elder daughter, Yaadhra, and the younger son, Jayaprakash. Meanwhile, his younger brother studied well and secured a good job in the Railways. The very next year, Agnee Raj got his brother married, completing the responsibilities his late father had left behind.

As Agnee Raj's children grew, his son Jayaprakash started speaking at around 3.5 years old. However, one day in August 2017, he began to stammer like his father.

Agnee Raj was entirely unprepared for this!

He never imagined that his son would end up stammering like him. The moment he thought about the insults and struggles he had faced in life and that his son would have to go through the same, the joy in his life turned into darkness in a single day.

He repeatedly told his son, *"Speak properly, don't stammer!"* But he didn't know how to help him. His son couldn't understand what he was trying to say. *How can a father and son, both stammerers, face society together?* He cried for many months without sleep.

He even contemplated death for both of them. He thought, *If I die, my wife and others will suffer. But can I kill just my son so he won't have to face this pain?* Then he wondered, *what sin this boy committed to be born as my son? Why should he die when I'm still alive?*

Instead of continuing in that dark, negative space, he decided there *must be a solution for stammering somewhere in this world. I will find it. I will dig it out.*

Agnee Raj was ready to pay any price for his son. He took him to many temples and hospitals, to psychiatrists, speech therapists, Siddha and Homeopathy doctors, godmen, spiritual healers, and more.

One day, while taking his son to an elderly speech therapist, he asked, *"Can I be cured?"*

The therapist replied, *"How a person speaks at 25 is how he'll speak for life. There won't be much improvement"* However, the therapist said he could help the son speak better.

Agnee Raj thought, "We've already lived our lives. Let at least my son speak fluently." So, he regularly took his son to therapy. However, there was no significant improvement in his son's speech.

Still, Agnee Raj did not give up his search for a solution to stammering.

One day, while browsing YouTube, he came across a video of Surya, who had trained under Dr. Manimaran and was now speaking fluently. From the first time he watched that video, Agnee Raj strongly believed: *My son can be cured too!*

He repeatedly watched that video like a beloved song, dreaming that his son would also one day speak like that.

Afraid to call Dr. Manimaran directly, he sent a WhatsApp message, explaining his son's stammering and asking for help. Immediately, Dr. Manimaran added him to the Tamil Super Speakers (TSS) group.

Only after six months did Agnee Raj begin to understand the activities of the TSS group. Until then, nobody in the group knew that someone by his name existed. Though he didn't participate in any activities, he didn't leave the group either. Even though his presence wasn't noticed, he continued observing the group's events quietly—which was his good fortune.

For stammerer Agnee Raj, the most significant turning point in life came on May 13, 2018, at a workshop held in Chennai.

His participation in the workshop was purely accidental. Though he knew about the event beforehand, he hesitated. Travelling 450 kilometres from Madurai to Chennai? Even if he went, what significant change could happen? That was his mindset. He was still unsure whether to go until 6 p.m. on the first day of the event.

At that moment, a TSS member named Yuvaraj called him and asked, "You're coming to the workshop tomorrow, right?" That was when Agnee Raj realised that people were expecting him. With that realisation, he quickly decided to attend, rushed home, informed his family, packed a bag and left for Chennai—his first trip to the city.

A few words about Yuvaraj: He trained alongside Surya at the stammering centre in Kottur, which Mr Manimaran led. Yuvaraj has now recovered 95% from his stammering, speaks fluently, works at a good company, and earns well.

At the workshop, Agnee Raj had the opportunity to meet Mr. Manimaran in person. That's when he learned that Manimaran wasn't a doctor but an engineer and was a person who stammers like Agnee Raj.

The workshop gave Agnee Raj many new insights into stammering. He realised that he was the reason his son stammered and that if he learned to speak fluently, his son could improve. From that moment on, he began speech practice with confidence for the sake of his son.

Due to his deep understanding of stammering, he started seeing improvement in his speech within just three months of practice. As his confidence grew, he practiced even more intensely. Like someone who unexpectedly finds a bride while lying idle on the porch, he too started speaking fluently within one year.

After that, he asked for speaking opportunities on various platforms and in group meetings. Why? Because now he understood his stammering.

In 2019, during a Pongal celebration, he spoke fluently on stage in front of his village people and received a big applause. When he got off the stage, his mother hugged and kissed him, saying, "Only now is my son speaking well." It was an unforgettable moment in Agnee Raj's life.

Today, even if Agnee Raj introduces himself as a stammer, no one is ready to believe him—that's how fluently he speaks now.

Following this, many good things began to happen in his life. After gaining a deep understanding of stammering through the TSS group, he wanted others to benefit too—and began implementing this vision.

He contacted people who stammer in Madurai and nearby districts, and for over 1.5 years, he consistently organised Self-Help Group meetings every Sunday in crowded public places like parks.

Not stopping there, during trips to tourist spots like Kodaikanal and Courtallam, he used loudspeakers in public places to speak about stammering, creating awareness among the public. This helped spread knowledge and contributed significantly to his speaking improvement.

Later, speaking with new people became part of Agnee Raj's routine. After joining the TSS group, he attended every single workshop without fail. He firmly believes that *attending just one workshop can give the benefit of six months of speech practice.*

In every workshop, he gained new insights into stammering. He also understood that meeting fellow stammerers, staying together for two or three days, dancing, singing, chatting, laughing, and enjoying themselves are deeply therapeutic and essential for people who stammer.

Nowadays, Agnee Raj is frequently invited to speak at school functions and public events. His life has once again turned toward happiness.

After three years of consistent speech practice, Agnee Raj started speaking fluently. Still, he continues his practice for two important reasons:

1. To inspire new TSS members, who often ask, "Do we have to practice for two or three years?"

2. To support his son, who only recently began speech practice.

You'll be surprised to know that Agnee Raj has completed over 2,000 days of practice!

He often regrets that he wasted 36 years stammering without knowing about these wonderful methods and that his son also began stammering because of it. He wonders how many others are unknowingly suffering like him and wishes this knowledge reached them, too.

Alongside Mr. Manimaran, he has learned the nuances of stammering and has committed to ensuring this service continues. He now actively supports the stammering community in every possible way.

Due to Agnee Raj's passionate dedication and selfless service to the TSS group, Mr. Manimaran appointed him as the Managing Director of the TSS group a few years ago—a role he continues to fulfil diligently.

One key activity in TSS is daily voice recording. Each day, a topic is given, and members must record a minimum of three minutes of audio and upload it to the group. Many stammerers believe they can't speak for even three minutes continuously. But those who began daily recordings, hesitant at first, slowly increased their speaking time—now, some can speak effortlessly for 30 minutes in a single go.

Agnee Raj is entirely responsible for this. For the past five years, he has provided daily topics, patiently listened to every member's voice recording, and given feedback—all consistently and without fail. Thanks to this daily practice initiative, many now speak fluently.

The Tamil Super Speakers (TSS) group is a self-help platform that removes the fear of speaking and helps people who stammer find their voice. It transformed Agnee Raj's life—and the lives of many others.

Inspired by Mr Manimaran's work, Agnee Raj committed to serving the stammering community for life, just like his mentor.

The Tamil Super Speakers train continues its journey. Some reach their destination, some get off midway, and some stay on and ride along. But the train keeps going, driven by one conductor or another. And so, the TSS journey will never stop.

Today, Agnee Raj's son is 11 years old. He has recently started his speech practice. Though he still stammers, he now speaks bravely and without fear. Agnee Raj firmly believes that his son will speak fluently in a few more years—and he's taken full responsibility for making that happen.

Now recovered from stammering, Agnee Raj lives a joyful life with his beautiful family, just like anyone else.

He loudly proclaims to the world:

"The secret to overcoming stammering is proper understanding, continuous practice, breaking hesitation, and speaking despite the stammer—everywhere."

"Stammering is not about stammering while speaking. Real stammering is staying silent, afraid you might stammer."

"Let's build a world free of stammering!"

Even while stammering, Agnee Raj worked hard in his business and lived a good life. Having started to speak fluently, he is also confident that his son will say well in a few years.

Would a Madurai native ever give up? Never!

He plans to expand his business and is exploring introducing new products in his shop. He believes with 100% certainty that he will also achieve great success in business.

Anyone wishing to overcome stammering can contact him anytime at Mobile 9345544950. He is always ready to help.

J. Agnee Raj – Madurai - Tamil Nadu

Email: jpnagneeuk@gmail.com

4

IF THERE IS A WILL, THERE IS A WAY

Originally from Tirunelveli, Sivasubramanian was born in 1950 in Kodaikanal into a large family. His father was a doctor and a senior official in the public health department. He retired in 1977 and later served as the Project Director of the Prevention of Blindness at Aravind Eye Hospital in Madurai, where he remained until he died in 2006. His mother was a homemaker. Siva had three sisters and three brothers, totalling seven children. He was the third child. The household also included cooks and helpers—his father maintained a large household. In Siva's family, his father, one sister, one brother, and Siva himself were all people who stammered.

Siva's mother passed away when he was just 17 while he was studying PUC (pre-university course). Despite this, his father did not remarry. He single-handedly raised all seven children, ensured they received a good education, arranged their marriages, and settled them into respectable lives.

Siva realised he stammered at around the age of 7. Since others in the family already stammered, he accepted it as a natural part of life. However, in school, he was shy and avoided speaking. He struggled to say "Present, sir" during attendance. When teachers

55

asked students to read aloud, he faced difficulties, but his teachers encouraged him to continue reading. Due to his father's government job, the family experienced frequent transfers, so Siva attended seven schools to complete his education.

When asked about his stammering, his father replied that there was no known medical treatment at the time (in the late 1950s). He advised Siva to read aloud from textbooks every morning. As a child, Siva didn't view his stammer as a significant flaw and usually interacted with people.

As he grew older, he began to push himself forward despite his stammer. He focused on academics, excelled in his studies, and earned a seat at Guindy Engineering College (now part of Anna University), which was affiliated with the University of Madras at the time. He pursued a degree in Civil Engineering. Due to his stammer, he was extremely shy and would skip class when he had to give seminars. He completed five years of study and obtained his engineering degree.

From a young age, Siva also suffered from asthma. Since the condition worsened outside Chennai and construction site pollution aggravated it, he decided to seek an indoor desk job in Chennai.

He secured a job as a lecturer at a government polytechnic college in Chennai. Though hesitant to accept a role that required regular public speaking, especially in front of students, he accepted it with courage.

Since he had a higher qualification than the students, he subconsciously developed a superiority complex, believing he was superior to them in all ways. This helped boost his confidence in teaching. The concept of "Big Me", as explained in Yuvraj's story, worked in his favour. Surprisingly, he didn't stammer much while teaching, especially in English, where his speech was more fluent.

Since government polytechnic lecturers are typically transferred every three years, Siva preferred a job-based in Chennai. When he got an offer from the Chennai Metropolitan Water Supply and Sewerage Board (CMWSSB), he took it immediately. His first post was Assistant Engineer in the Operations and Maintenance department, a role that involved interacting with the public and communicating frequently over the phone with superiors. His prior teaching experience helped him adapt well.

Two years into his job at the Water Board, Siva got married. By then, his speech had significantly improved, so he did not disclose it to his future wife. However, he did share details about his asthma. Fortunately, her father also had asthma, so they were understanding. Siva and his wife were married in 1981.

His wife is also an engineer and retired as a Superintending Engineer from the Tamil Nadu Electricity Board.

While at the Water Board, Siva met a young engineer named Manimaran. Impressed by Manimaran's sincerity and kindness, they developed a strong friendship that lasted 44 years and is still going strong. After retiring in 2013, Manimaran began dedicating his full time to helping people who stammer, offering selfless support. Inspired by this, Siva also started contributing to the cause. Until two years ago, he regularly participated in speech workshops in Chennai, giving motivational speeches.

Due to age and health, Siva no longer attends in person. However, he was amazed to learn that platforms like WhatsApp could also be used effectively for social good.

Regarding his family, Siva's wife is deeply religious. She has visited hundreds of temples across India and rarely misses a day without visiting one. They have one daughter, who is also an engineer. She lives in England with her engineering husband and their 12-year-old son.

FINAL MESSAGE FROM SIVASUBRAMANIAN

"Overcoming stammering requires mental courage and determination. Finding a mentor like Manimaran is a great blessing for today's generation. I hope everyone uses his guidance effectively, overcomes stammering, and lives better."

S. Sivasubramanian – Chennai - Tamil Nadu

Email:_siva1350@yahoo.co.in

5

TALK SLOWLY USING BODY LANGUAGE

My name is Karunyamoorthy. I was born in 1967 in Tambaram, near Chennai. My father worked as a Village Munsif in Tambaram, a position now known as Village Administrative Officer (VAO). My mother was a homemaker. I have five siblings—an elder brother and four younger sisters. I was the only one in my family with a stammer; the rest spoke fluently. I have had this speech difficulty since childhood. I studied in Tambaram until 10th grade.

During my school days, even answering the attendance roll call was a challenge for me. While all the other students would confidently say, "Present, Sir," I would raise my hand instead of saying it aloud. My classmates would laugh at me. However, my teacher understood my speech difficulty. Instead of waiting for me to struggle, he checked if I raised my hand when my name was called.

Even when I knew the answers to the teacher's questions, I was too afraid to speak due to my stammer. So, I would say, "I don't know", even when I knew. For students who answered "I don't know", the teacher would assign a task—writing a Thirukkural (a Tamil couplet) ten times and reading it aloud ten times at home.

59

This is what sparked my deep interest in Tamil. In 12ᵗʰ grade, I scored 75 marks in Tamil. Back then, 75 marks were equivalent to 95 by today's standards!

Some students used to mock me for my stammer. But most of my classmates supported me, and my teachers were very encouraging.

My father took me to a doctor to help me overcome my stammering. The doctor asked me to stand in front of a mirror and practice speaking. I did this for six months, but my stammering only worsened instead of improving. Another time, my father took me to a Siddha doctor. This doctor advised me to eat gooseberry (Amla) coated with honey for a mandalam (48 days). I followed his advice, but my speech did not improve.

Later, I joined Nidhi Higher Secondary School in Alandur for my 11ᵗʰ grade. On the first day of class, we were asked to introduce ourselves. I struggled a lot and stammered heavily while saying my name. The teacher did not let me go quickly. He kept asking me questions and made me speak for five minutes. Some students laughed at me, but many of them were supportive.

After completing school, I joined SIVET College near Tambaram and took a B.Sc. in Mathematics. I chose Mathematics because other courses required more speaking, whereas I wouldn't have to speak much in Mathematics—just numbers!

On the first day of college, we were again asked to introduce ourselves. Interestingly, even the mathematics professor had a stammer. Because of this, he sympathised with me and treated me with great kindness. I graduated from college in 1988.

After completing my degree, I stayed at home for only four months. Then, in late 1988, I joined my uncle's finance company as an accountant. I worked there for 16 years.

At that time, landline phones were the only mode of business communication. I had to speak with many customers over the phone. My uncle insisted that I improve my speaking skills, as it would be difficult to work if I couldn't communicate well.

MARRIAGE PROPOSAL CHALLENGES

Meanwhile, my marriage proposal process began. The first time we went to see a bride, we spent almost an hour there. But I spoke only a few words. The bride's family felt the groom was not speaking correctly, so they rejected the proposal.

I had already informed the bride's family about my stammering in advance for the second proposal. They didn't mind, and we got married in the year 2000.

POST-MARRIAGE EXPERIENCES

After marriage, whenever my wife and I went out, I faced problems while buying tickets. One time, we were travelling by train from Tambaram to Mambalam. Instead of asking for a ticket to Mambalam, I said Kodambakkam. My wife was surprised and asked, "Aren't we going to Mambalam? Why did you buy a ticket to Kodambakkam?" I casually replied, "The ticket charge for both Mambalam and Kodambakkam is the same."

Another time, while travelling by bus to Mangadu, I asked for a ticket to Poonamallee instead. Seeing this, my wife took charge of buying tickets whenever we travelled. She fully supported me through my stammering struggles.

DISCOVERING A STAMMERING SOLUTION

One day, I came across an article in the Dinamalar Weekly Magazine (Tamil) by Mr. Balasubramaniam titled "Seven Days to Overcome Stammering". The article did not mention his phone number, so I had to call the Dinamalar office to get it. Since I was a stammerer, I asked a friend to call the Dinamalar office and ask for Mr. Balasubramaniam's phone number. My friend got the number, and I called Mr. Balasubramaniam myself.

I stammered a lot while speaking to him. However, he understood my struggle because he was also a former stammerer. He asked me to write a letter explaining my problem. So, I wrote a postcard detailing my stammering issue and sent it to his address. After reading my letter, he replied, informing me that he would visit Chennai next month. He asked me to meet him at a hotel in Anna Salai.

JOINING THE COURSE IN MADURAI

At first, my mother did not want me to go to Madurai for this course. She told me,

"You speak well enough! Why do you want to go to Madurai unnecessarily?" However, my wife supported me and said, "If you believe that attending this course in Madurai will solve your problem, then go and participate."

Following her advice, I went to the hotel in Chennai on the scheduled date. Around 10 people had gathered there; that was the first time I met Mr. Manimaran.

(A small detail I'd like to mention here is that Manimaran's father was living in Tambaram. He was also an engineer, just like Manimaran. I had heard about him through one of my relatives, but I only realised that Manimaran was his son while attending the course.)

Eventually, only five people attended the course. The seven-day training went on well.

SPEECH TRAINING EXPERIENCE

As detailed in Mr. Manimaran's story, by the final day, all of us were speaking fluently without stammering. Mr. Balasubramaniam advised us to continue the speech practice until we could speak fluently.

At first, I practiced consistently for six months. Occasionally, I attended the weekly meetings conducted by Mr. Manimaran near the Gandhi statue at Marina Beach. However, due to personal family issues, I could not continue my speech practice regularly. As a result, my stammering worsened again.

ADOPTING A CHILD

Along with my speech struggles, my wife and I faced another challenge—even after five years of marriage, we did not have a child. I believed that my increased stammering was due to the stress from multiple problems.

In 2005, we decided to adopt a baby girl from an orphanage. While giving her up for adoption, the orphanage advised us, "A few years later, you should tell your daughter the truth about her adoption." Now, our daughter is studying in college. We revealed the truth to her two years ago.

OVERCOMING STAMMERING THROUGH CONTINUOUS PRACTICE

I started practicing speech exercises to improve my fluency. Although I couldn't practice consistently, I continued off and on. Later, I also learned and practiced breathing exercises. I made book reading a daily habit. Even today, I continue to do breathing exercises regularly.

Meanwhile, I attended self-help meetings conducted by Mr. Manimaran at the YWCA and participated in several workshops held in Chennai.

FINANCIAL STRUGGLES AND THEIR IMPACT ON MY SPEECH

Even though I had a significant amount of ancestral property, legal and financial issues prevented me from selling it. From

2016 to 2018, I struggled financially. The stress worsened my stammering. My wife stood by my side during that difficult time, providing constant support.

In 2018, I finally sold my ancestral property and received substantial money. Using part of this money, I purchased land near Padappai. Now, I am engaged in organic farming there.

This experience helped me understand something important—when we face financial difficulties, our stress levels increase, which worsens stammering. However, once I became financially stable, my stammering reduced significantly.

YOGA AND HELPING OTHERS

I started attending several yoga classes and eventually began teaching yoga myself. I now conduct yoga classes for about 1.5 hours every day. Through constant speaking in these classes, my speech greatly improved.

Today, I can confidently say that I no longer stammer. It only happens occasionally when I am unwell; otherwise, I speak fluently.

I now teach yoga and breathing exercises to many people. Those suffering from frequent colds, insomnia, headaches, and heart problems come to me for guidance. I provide breathing exercises to them completely free of charge. One person with Parkinson's disease came to me for help. After practicing the breathing techniques, I taught him, he returned to work within two months.

Today, I am happily enjoying life, helping others, and living with gratitude.

I want to mention an incident three days ago on Shivaratri (26.02.2025). Near our house, the Shivaratri festival was celebrated grandly. To control the crowd of devotees, we arranged for 15 policemen. I guided them on how to manage the crowd.

My advice to those who stammer is that stammering is a mind-related issue. You need to plant the thought in your mind that you can speak fluently. Of course, it is not that easy. I could only talk fluently on the fourth day of Mr. Balasubramanian's course. That was when the strong belief settled deep in my subconscious that I could talk well. Similarly, you must practice speech training consistently to speak fluently.

You must use a technique that works for you to improve your speech. Once you start speaking fluently, self-confidence will automatically develop within you.

Another important point I want to emphasise is that you must train yourself to speak slowly, using head movements. I know that speaking slowly is not easy. But if you consciously remind yourself frequently that you must talk slowly and practice it consistently, it will soon become a natural habit.

As I mentioned earlier, financially stable people tend to experience less tension. When there is less stress, it becomes easier to speak fluently.

Overcome your stammering and take control of your life.

The sky will be yours!

K. Karunyamoorthy – Tambaram - Tamil Nadu

Email: kaarunsahana@gmail.com

6

REACHING NEW YORK WAS HIS BLESSING

Francis was born in 1969 in Manapparai, near Tiruchirappalli. His father was a farmer, and while his mother was a homemaker, she also helped her husband with farming activities. Francis has three siblings—an elder brother, a younger brother, and a younger sister. He has had a stammering issue since childhood, and his father also had the same condition.

Francis completed his school education in Malayapatti, a village near Manapparai. Like most people with stammering, he also faced difficulties during the daily roll call at school. However, he managed to get through it by saying whatever came to his mind at that moment, such as "Yes, Sir," "Present, Sir," or "Here, Sir." Fortunately, neither his teachers nor classmates made fun of him.

He completed his Mechanical Engineering degree in 1991 in Keeranur, near Pudukottai. Even during college, he was never mocked or bullied for his stammering. Though he struggled while presenting seminars, his lecturers and classmates were understanding and supportive. Even during his final-year project viva, the professors were cooperative. Unlike many with stammering issues, Francis completed his school and college education without ridicule or humiliation.

Since Francis' parents were not highly educated, and his father also had a stammering issue, they never considered it a serious problem. As a result, he was never taken to a doctor for treatment. In 1991, after completing his engineering degree, he suffered from another health issue, which forced him to stay at home for four years to undergo treatment.

FRANCIS' JOURNEY IN OVERCOMING STAMMERING

In 1995, Francis consulted a speech therapy specialist in Tiruchirappalli. The specialist taught him exercises for the mouth and tongue and instructed him to practice them regularly. Francis diligently followed these exercises for three months, spending ₹2000 on therapy. However, he saw no improvement and eventually gave up, believing that his stammering could not be cured.

In 1996, he started working in a small company in Tiruchirappalli. The following year (1997), he married a woman from a family he knew. Since both families were familiar, his wife's family was already aware of his stammering issue. His wife has been supportive of him ever since.

In 1998, Francis moved to Chennai for searching a better job. However, big companies refused to hire him due to his stammering problem. Determined not to remain jobless, he took up a Data Entry Operator job with a salary of ₹3000. At this point, he became serious about finding a solution to his speech issue.

While searching for remedies, he came across a newspaper advertisement about a training program conducted by Mr. Balasubramanian. (For those who have read this book, Mr. Balasubramanian's success story is featured in the first chapter. His efforts in overcoming stammering are well documented there.)

In 2000, Francis attended Mr. Balasubramanian's training camp, which Mr. Manimaran also participated in. Francis had the most severe stammering among the attendees. As mentioned in Manimaran's success story, Francis, like all others, could speak fluently by the last day of the training. He was overjoyed, believing that his stammering had finally disappeared.

However, fate had different plans for him...

A RENEWED COMMITMENT TO OVERCOMING STAMMERING

As Manimaran described in his success story, following his advice, a group of five individuals from Chennai met every Sunday at 5 PM at Marina Beach. They gathered to share their progress and support each other in overcoming their stammering.

However, Manimaran's health deteriorated after two months, and he stopped attending these meetings. As a result, the group eventually disbanded, and each member went their separate ways. Unfortunately, Francis also stopped his speech practice, and his stammering worsened over time.

REUNITING WITH MANIMARAN

After about six months, Francis and Manimaran reconnected. By then, Manimaran's health had improved, but since he had also stopped practising speech exercises, he had relapsed into stammering.

When they met again, Manimaran suggested:

"Both of us have started stammering again. We find it difficult to practice alone at home for an hour. Instead, let's meet daily at Marina Beach in the evening and practice together."

(At this point, readers must understand that this happened in 2000. Back then, mobile phones were just being introduced, and

only the wealthy could afford them. There were no WhatsApp groups or support communities like today. Overcoming stammering alone without a support system was extremely rare. Additionally, during those times, there was no awareness about openly accepting stammering. If someone stammered while practising, they would often feel discouraged. Only in 2009, when The Indian Stammering Association (TISA) promote the idea that accepting stammering openly could help reduce mental stress and improve speech confidence.)

A MONTH OF INTENSIVE SPEECH PRACTICE

Francis agreed with Manimaran's suggestion and started meeting daily at Marina Beach in the evenings. They would sit 100 feet apart on the sand and practice speech exercises for an hour.

They continued this routine for a month. However, due to Manimaran's increasing work commitments, he was unable to attend the sessions regularly. Eventually, the Marina Beach speech practice sessions ended. That one month of speech practice at Marina Beach brought Francis a significant realisation about life.

Francis was already a True Christian—a man of prayer with unwavering faith in God. One day, Manimaran handed Francis a copy of "The Power of Positive Thinking" by Norman Vincent Peale. At that time, this book was extremely popular. Peale, a highly respected pastor in America, emphasised the importance of positive thoughts in achieving success. After reading the book, Francis became convinced that positive thinking leads to outstanding achievements.

A RAINY EVENING AT MARINA BEACH

As usual, Francis and Manimaran were practising their speech exercises at Marina Beach one evening. The sky suddenly darkened and looked like it was about to rain.

Manimaran asked,

"What do we do if it starts raining now?"

Francis pointed to a small police booth in the distance and said,

"We can take shelter there." (In Marina Beach, there are very few places to shelter when it rains.)

As expected, heavy rain began to pour within 30 minutes. Francis and Manimaran ran toward the police booth, but by the time they reached it, around 20 other people had already gathered around it, trying to escape from the rain.

Two policemen shut the door inside the booth to keep themselves dry. Soon, strong winds started blowing, and rain water began splashing onto everyone standing outside.

Manimaran sighed and said,

"Now we are completely stuck in the rain!"

Francis, however, remained calm and confident. He said,

"Don't worry, sir. I have already prayed. Just watch—one of the policemen inside will call only the two of us in."

To everyone's surprise, one of the policemen inside opened the door within a minute and called only Francis and Manimaran to come in.

Once inside, the policeman pointed to two chairs and asked them to sit down. The booth was tiny, with only two chairs available.

After the rain stopped, Francis and Manimaran thanked the policemen and left.

Manimaran was shocked. Though the incident was minor, he couldn't understand why the policeman only called them inside, leaving everyone else standing outside in the rain. This event left a lasting impression on both of them.

One day, Francis told Manimaran,

"Sir, one day, I am going to America!"

Manimaran smiled and wished him good luck. But deep inside, he felt pity for Francis.

"Poor guy! He still hasn't found a good job. He struggles to speak fluently in English. He still stammers. Why does he even have this big dream?"

In 2005, Francis moved to Bangalore in search of a job. He joined a software company and worked hard to earn a good reputation there. Over time, he learned to manage his stammering, which significantly improved his speech.

Due to his dedication and skills, the company selected Francis for an on-site opportunity. And guess where? The on-site location was New York, USA! When Manimaran heard the news, his happiness knew no bounds. Francis had immense faith in positive thinking, but he also knew how to apply it in real life.

LIFE IN THE USA & CAREER GROWTH

Francis worked in New York City for two years. In 2010 he returned to Bangalore and continued working for the same software company until 2019.

By 2015, Medical Coding was becoming an emerging field. Francis developed a keen interest in it and started learning through part-time courses. With passion and dedication, he mastered every detail of Medical Coding. After gaining expertise, he even started teaching others. Once he became a certified expert, Francis resigned from his software job and joined a Medical Coding company.

Francis' journey proves that with hard work, perseverance, and positive thinking, one can overcome any challenge—even stammering—and achieve great success.

Even today, Francis continues to work at the same Medical Coding company. But now, he is the company's "all-in-all." Under his leadership, 25 employees work, and he earns a six-figure salary.

FAMILY & PERSONAL LIFE

Francis has a son, born in 2000. His son graduated as an engineer and works in a software company in Bangalore. Unlike his father, he speaks fluently.

FRANCIS' ADVICE TO YOUNG PEOPLE WHO STAMMER

When asked what advice he has for young people who stammer, Francis simply said:

"Forgive those who mock you with all your heart. That way, you won't have any mental stress. And when there is no stress, you can speak well."

P. Francis – Bengaluru - Karnataka

Email: famuthan@gmail.com

7

PHOTOGRAPHER TO THE DIRECTOR OF PHOTOGRAPHY

Raja Bhattacharjee was born in 1971 in Tambaram, near Chennai. His father ran a workshop manufacturing electrical spare part, and his mother was a homemaker. His parents were originally from West Bengal and had moved to Chennai around 70 years ago. Raja grew up in a large joint family with two elder sisters, one elder brother, one younger sister, and extended family members, including uncles, totalling about 15 people.

Raja had a stammer from a very young age. His elder brother also stammered. He completed his schooling in Tambaram. Like many who stammer, he faced typical challenges. For instance, during daily roll call, he would vary his response each day, saying "Yes, sir," "Present, sir," or "Vandhen, sir" (meaning "I came, sir")—whichever he could manage fluently that day. He formed a small circle of close friends and avoided interacting with others, creating a "comfort zone" around himself.

Teachers would ask him questions in class, but when he tried to answer, he would stammer, and they would quickly move on to the next student. He couldn't even read two lines properly during classroom reading sessions, so he was often told to sit down.

His father wanted him to study engineering, but Raja wasn't interested due to the field's communication-heavy nature. Still, he respected his father's wishes and appeared for multiple engineering entrance exams, though he didn't perform well intentionally. He told his father he loved physics and eventually joined SIVET College near Tambaram to pursue a BSc in Physics.

During college, he joined the National Cadet Corps (NCC). Once, the NCC master asked him to train others for Republic Day. Afraid to give commands due to his stammer, he feigned illness and dropped out of the NCC. Even in college, he kept to a small group of friends, staying within his comfort zone so his stammer didn't become a significant issue.

Raja graduated with a Bachelor of Science degree in Physics in 1992. After graduation, he became interested in joining the film industry. When his father learned of this, he introduced Raja to a film producer he knew. The producer advised against entering the film field due to the slim chances of success and said that even if one succeeds, it might only be after 40—if at all.

Raja then took a computer course during the early days of computer popularity. He learned that graphics could be created using computers. Inspired by Marine engineering students from Kolkata and Agartala, he developed an interest in the field. However, the head of the institute, a naval officer, told Raja that this career wouldn't suit someone who stammers and that other professions might be a better fit for him.

Raja would go to his father's workshop near their home during school holidays. After graduation, he continued helping there occasionally.

Later, he enrolled in courses such as Graphics and CAD, with his mind still set on entering the film industry. At that time, the renowned Penta Four company taught a popular software called STUDIO. Raja studied there and even got a job at Penta Four.

Between 1996 and 1998, Raja learned 3D graphics and finally began stepping out of his comfort zone. Had he done this earlier, he might've worked on addressing his stammer. But staying in his comfort zone for so long meant he never tried to overcome it. Once, his father took both Raja and his elder brother to a wellness centre that used Ayurvedic, acupuncture, and breathing therapy. But it didn't help.

While working at Penta Four, Raja fell in love with and married a woman in 1999. At the time of marriage, he was unemployed while his wife worked. She had studied for a Bachelor of Arts in Fine Arts.

Raja made his first solo trip—to Ooty—without friends. A person who had studied in the UK had started a film institute there. Raja joined and completed the course in 2001. Afterwards, instead of returning to Chennai, he left for Mumbai with a friend, hoping to find work. But his elder brother was diagnosed with cancer, forcing Raja to come to Chennai frequently.

By 2003, his brother's condition worsened, and Raja had to stay in Chennai. Still hoping to find opportunities in the film industry, he tried his luck in Bangalore—closer to Chennai—but didn't find suitable work there either. His brother passed away in 2005, and Raja was forced to return to Chennai permanently.

Now married and under financial pressure, he started his own photography business, specialising in weddings and family events and creating photo albums. This brought in a decent income.

Around this time, he began thinking seriously about addressing his stammer. He heard about Dr. Sachin and attended a week-long TISA workshop in Dehradun. There, he gained a complete understanding of stammering. Dr. Sachin asked him, "What would you do if you could choose any job you liked?" Raja said, "I love certain fields, but I haven't pursued them because of my stammer." Dr. Sachin replied, "You must do exactly what you find most difficult. You shouldn't always stay in your comfort zone."

In Chennai, Raja found an ad about a five-day film-related course at IIT. He joined it alone. About 200 participants attended from various states. Eight South Indian participants, including Raja, formed a group. They began making short films, and he naturally became the cameraman since Raja owned a video camera.

Meanwhile, in Chennai, Mr. Manimaran used to conduct weekly self-help group meetings at the YWCA International Guest House. Raja began attending whenever possible, establishing a bond with Mr. Manimaran. Raja, his wife, and Mr. Manimaran attended two TISA national conferences—one in Bhubaneswar, Odisha, and the other in Coorg, Karnataka.

The eight-person team participated in a show called "Tomorrow's Director" on Kalaignar TV. Later, a Telugu-speaking teammate helped Raja get a job as Director of Photography (DOP) for a Telugu film titled *Ticket* in 2016, although the film was never released in India.

In 2017, he served as the Director of Photography (DOP) for another Telugu film, *Kaaram Dosa*, which was officially released. That marked his first credited work. Since then, he has worked as the cinematographer on seven released films:

* *Pyaar Prem Kadhal*

* *Kazhugu 2*

* *Idiot*

* *Naan Mirugamaai Maara*

✶ *Ninaivellam Neeyada*

✶ *Tharunam*

Two more films are pending release.

RAJA'S MESSAGE TO PEOPLE WHO STAMMER

"Don't always stay in your comfort zone. If you do, you'll never take the steps to overcome stammering. If you treat your stammer as a problem, it will always remain one. However, you won't move forward if you continue focusing on the problem. Instead, build expertise in a field you love. For argument's sake, will you immediately get a good job if your stammer goes away tomorrow? Grow your talent and uniqueness. When you have talent, no one can ignore or reject you."

"Your talent alone will determine your life."

Raja Bhattacharjee – Chennai - Tamil Nadu

Email: rajabhatta@gmail.com

8

IT'S NEVER TOO LATE

Chittibabu was born in 1977 in the quiet town of Bhuvanagiri in Tamil Nadu's Cuddalore district. His father was a farmer, and his mother a homemaker. He was the youngest in a large family that struggled financially, with an elder brother and a younger sister. Despite hardships, his parents deeply valued education. His mother, a pillar of strength, often said, *"Education is life."* Inspired by her words, he began studying in a government school, where the midday meal program and free uniforms played a significant role in his early education.

He studied up to 10th grade at a government school in Bhuvanagiri. After that, he aspired to take a polytechnic course. However, low scores shattered that dream. Determined to find an alternative path, he chose a vocational stream in his higher secondary school. But fate had a different plan. His headmaster, Mr. Santhanam, felt his small stature might make vocational training physically difficult and encouraged him to switch to the computer science stream. That decision turned out to be a life-changing one.

During school, Chittibabu didn't think much about his stammering. But when he joined BSc Computer Science at AVC College in Mayiladuthurai, he began to face the harsh realities of his speech disorder. Hostel life added its own set of challenges.

Still, he excelled academically. His elder brother, Mr. Pugazhendhi, supported him financially throughout his college studies.

Later, Chittibabu joined Annamalai University in Chidambaram for an MCA degree. However, his speech difficulties hindered him, especially during seminars and presentations. One incident remains etched in his memory—he was so afraid to speak at a college welcome event for seniors that he pretended to be unwell and skipped it. He regretted that decision deeply afterwards.

In 1999, Chittibabu moved to Chennai. Though skilled in computers, his limited English proficiency made him feel insecure. His coding abilities helped him secure his first job at a reputed company. He spent two successful years in the corporate world. But a painful incident broke his spirit—he was denied an onsite opportunity because of his stammering. His team lead bluntly asked, "How will you speak fluently with clients?" While colleagues with lesser technical knowledge were chosen for the role, he was rejected.

Determined to overcome his stammering, Chittibabu attended a one-week course that taught him to speak slowly and stretch syllables. But applying it in real life wasn't easy. Despite his technical strengths, he was often rejected during interviews due to HR concerns about how he would handle client conversations.

One particularly hurtful moment came when a senior manager acknowledged his skills but still rejected him, fearing his stammer would harm the company's reputation.

Chittibabu realised that his professional growth would be slow. On a personal level, finding a life partner wasn't easy either. Many families rejected him because of his stammering. But eventually, his steady job led to a marriage proposal. He got married in 2005. The bride's family was informed about his speech disorder beforehand, but his wife never treated it as an issue and never brought it up.

An opportunity in the United States allowed Chittibabu to showcase his technical expertise, though he still lagged behind his peers in career growth. When he joined a new company in 2010, he began seriously seeking solutions to his stammering. By chance, he came across Mr. V. Manimaran through a Yahoo group. That random encounter led him to the Tamil Super Speakers (TSS) self-help group. There, he learned the importance of accepting his stammer and developed the courage to face the world confidently.

Initially, Chittibabu didn't fully commit to speech practice. But in 2019, he attended a workshop for people who stammer, and Mr. Manimaran's speech reignited a spark within him. From that moment, he resumed regular speech practice—and continues to do so to this day. He now speaks fluently 95% of the time, and more importantly, doesn't worry if he occasionally stumbles.

A significant turning point came when Mr. Manimaran asked Chittibabu to record a video showcasing his speech progress for YouTube. Chittibabu had his son record the video and send it to Mr Manimaran. From then on, he began accepting his stammer more openly. That video remains on Mr. Manimaran's channel. It not only showed a man striving for progress but also a supportive family standing by him. His children, having seen him practice daily, viewed his stammering as just another trait of their father—not as a flaw.

In 2022, with renewed hope, Chittibabu took on a challenging role in a new company. He actively participated in TSS workshops and WhatsApp groups, refining his techniques, including "pausing" and the "Big Me" concept. As his life progressed, his persistence paid off, and he became an inspiration to others facing similar struggles.

Today, Chittibabu is a symbol of resilience. His journey, marked by moments of despair and triumph, highlights the power of self-acceptance and determination. Surrounded by a loving family and trusted friends, he proves that success is not a destination but a journey. His story reminds us that the most significant victories in life often come from conquering our deepest fears.

After joining TSS, Chittibabu experienced significant personal growth. His listening and observation skills improved significantly. He could express himself more effectively, which strengthened both his speech and communication abilities. Over time, he shed his fear of stammering and began speaking openly with colleagues, friends, and relatives.

Since joining the TSS group, he secured a higher-level role in a new position and successfully managed a large team. He developed the confidence to interact comfortably with both new and senior colleagues. All of these gains came from his continued engagement with the TSS group.

Today, Chittibabu lives happily in Chennai with his wife, 16-year-old son, and 12-year-old daughter, earning a handsome salary.

Chittibabu expresses his heartfelt gratitude to Mr. Manimaran and Mr. Agniraj for creating awareness about stammering and guiding him with speech therapy. The TSS group, managed selflessly by these two, is a free, service-oriented platform that helps individuals overcome stammering. He thanks them sincerely for their priceless support.

FINAL ADVICE FROM CHITTIBABU TO PEOPLE WHO STAMMER

✳ Focus entirely on your work.

✳ Continuously update and upgrade your skills.

✳ Keep improving your English proficiency.

❋   Don't wait to overcome stammering to start your duties—start now.

❋   Don't constantly think about stammering. Do what's needed to improve, and then shift your focus to other important aspects of life.

S. Chittibabu – Chennai - Tamil Nadu

Email: chittbabu.sa@gmail.com

9

CHENNAI TO SOUTH AFRICA

A CHILDHOOD OF STAMMERING AND SILENT STRUGGLES

I, Vinoth Kumar, was born in 1991 in Ranipet district. My father worked as an accountant in a brick manufacturing factory, and my mother is a homemaker. I have an elder brother. I am the only one in my family who stammers.

When I began to speak, the words I wanted never came out quickly. My childhood was marked by hesitation, despair, and numerous awkward moments. Every sentence I tried to speak felt like climbing a mountain. But before reaching the summit, I would often fall back down.

At home, my parents were supportive. Still, they couldn't fully understand the depth of my struggle. The outside world, however, was merciless. My school days weren't just about speech—they became a constant battle due to the reactions it provoked. Every time I tried to speak in class, laughter would echo in my ears long after it had stopped.

A LAUGHING "PLAY BOX"

People around me didn't see my struggle—I was just entertainment to them. I became a sort of "play box"—whenever I tried to speak,

83

I triggered laughter. It wasn't just children; even some adults enjoyed how I spoke.

At family gatherings, I would begin conversations nervously. If someone asked me a question, I knew exactly what would follow—a pause, a stammer, and then waves of laughter. I just wanted to run away.

THE PRESSURE TO SPEAK

When I received my 10th-grade exam results, I felt excited and anxious. But more than the scores, I feared something else—talking about them. Relatives and neighbours asked, "How many marks did you get?"

I held a copy of my mark sheet in my hand. Instead of saying my scores, I would show it to them. Some would nod and move on. But others would insist that I speak. "What's there to hide? Say it out loud. We want to hear it from you!" Their words hurt me more than my stammering ever did. I wanted to scream, "You don't understand my problem!" But I couldn't. I stayed silent instead.

AN UNEXPECTED TEACHER: AN ELDERLY MAN AND A NEWSPAPER

One day, something unexpected happened. A nearby elderly man used to read the newspaper every morning. He had recently undergone eye surgery and couldn't read independently.

One evening, as I walked by, he called out to me. "Son, could you read the newspaper for me?" I hesitated. Me? Read aloud? In front of someone? But something about his request felt different. He wasn't testing me. He wasn't mocking me. He wanted to listen.

With trembling hands, I picked up the newspaper and began to read. The words still faltered, but I continued. The old man listened patiently. There was no laughter, no comments, just calm, quiet patience.

I read for him day by day. And one day, something strange happened. I realised I was reading a little better than before. My stammer wasn't as intense. It was a small change, but for the first time in my life, I felt a tiny seed of confidence beginning to sprout within me.

I TRIED EVERY TECHNIQUE I READ IN BOOKS

(Before this, I had already tried everything others had suggested.)

* Placing a small pebble under my tongue while speaking

* Holding a long pepper in my mouth, believing it would magically smoothen my speech

* Breathing exercises

* Speaking slowly

* Completely avoiding some difficult words

Nothing worked. Some of these experiments made me appear more ridiculous, leading to further mockery and humiliation. By the time I was 17, I was exhausted. *"Is this how my life is going to be forever?"* But somewhere deep inside, a small fire kept burning. That's when my real journey began...

FROM TAMIL TO ENGLISH: A NEW STRUGGLE

My world revolved around Tamil. Every subject, every exam, every conversation—everything felt natural in my Tamil-my mother tongue. I never had to guess words or worry about whether I was saying them right.

Then came college: engineering. For many, it's a dream. It was a challenge for me—and not just because of the subjects. For the first time, I was thrown into an English-speaking environment.

Every class, every lecture, every textbook—everything was in English.

If speaking in Tamil was difficult, speaking in English was even more so. The words refused to come out. The harder I tried, the more my confidence shattered.

THE SILENT STUDENT

It didn't take me long to realise that the easiest way to avoid embarrassment was to stay silent.

Stage events? Avoided.

Group discussions? Ignored.

Class questions? I pretended like they weren't even asked.

Even when I knew the answer, I kept my mouth shut. Because knowing something and saying it out loud are two completely different things. As soon as I opened my mouth, my stammer would send me reeling. I would return to that same old place—watched, judged, and labelled. I became the student who never spoke. Professors eventually stopped expecting answers from me.

THE FINAL FEAR – VIVA AND PROJECT PRESENTATIONS

One of the biggest fears for engineering students, even those who speak well, is the viva exam and project presentations. For me, they were more than fear—they were torture.

Viva exams require you to stand before a professor and answer technical questions on the spot. My problem was not the lack of knowledge—I knew the answers. I couldn't speak them out loud.

One particular viva still haunts me. As usual, I entered the room, nervous and tense. The professor looked at me, waiting for an answer. I opened my mouth—nothing came out.

He just paused and stammered, and an awkward silence ensued. After a few seconds, he sighed and asked, "Can you at least speak in Tamil?"

It was a relieving moment, but at the same time, it wasn't very comfortable. There I was—an engineering student—unable to articulate my project in the language I had been taught.

Upon realising how much I struggled, some professors stopped asking me questions altogether.

To many, that might seem like mercy. But to me, it was worse than failure. They weren't ignoring me because I didn't know the answers. They ignored me because they thought I couldn't answer. But I don't blame them—it wasn't their fault.

Campus Interview Day

Some colleges have a tactic to showcase "100% placement" rates. To ensure even weaker students get jobs, they invite call centre companies. It's an open secret—if you don't get a better job, at least you'll get some job, and the college can proudly claim "100% placements!"

But guess what happened? I was the only one who didn't get selected. Yes, I couldn't make it through even in a call centre interview. The interview was straightforward—basic English, some customer service questions, and a brief test to assess our fluency.

I knew this was my weak spot. Still, I went in with hope. Within minutes, I knew it wasn't going well. I stammered. I paused for long moments. Sometimes, I just stayed silent. When the results came out, everyone got selected—except me. Even those with no technical knowledge, coding skills, or real experience were selected.

I left that interview hall shattered, without a job, no confidence, and the same old speech issue, even after completing my engineering degree. And because the interview was in English, my stammering was at its worst.

A NEW BEGINNING

Before I even finished college, I was convinced that my future was already ruined.

How would I ever succeed if I couldn't clear a simple interview? For years, I had fought with my stammer. By the time I completed my engineering degree, I felt like I had lost that battle. But the story didn't end there. Because sometimes, failure is not the end—it's the beginning of something bigger.

FRIENDS – SILENT SUPPORTERS

If there was one blessing in my life, it was my friends. They never treated me differently. They never saw me as less because of my stammer. Without even realising it, they often became my voice in many situations. Whenever we went out—to a shop, a restaurant, or even to book a ticket—they spoke on my behalf.

At first, it felt convenient. I didn't have to struggle. I didn't have to face awkward moments.

Most importantly, I didn't have to feel embarrassed. They would place the order for me if we were at a hotel. If we were in a store, they'd ask me what I needed and speak to the shopkeeper. If someone asked me a question, they would answer on my behalf.

I thought it was helping me. And yes, in some ways, it was. But what I didn't realise at the time was—instead of moving forward, I was hiding.

SPEAK, SPEAK, SPEAK!

Looking back now, one crucial truth has become clear to me—if I had faced my fear and chosen to speak despite the stammer, I could have overcome it before I turned 20.

My humble advice to everyone struggling with a speech disorder is: "Even if you stammer, keep speaking!" Avoiding speech makes stammering worse. I relied on others to speak on my behalf. I hid behind my silence and tried to skip over conversations. It gave me temporary comfort.

However, in the long run, it ultimately delayed my growth and prolonged my struggle. I could have gained confidence much sooner if I had pushed myself forward.

STRUGGLES IN EVERYDAY LIFE

The difficulties weren't limited to college. Even the most ordinary, day-to-day tasks turned into terrifying nightmares for me.

* Buying a bus ticket? I struggled to say the name of my stop. The conductor would lose patience.

* Ordering food at a hotel? I avoided it altogether. I'd let my friends order for me.

* Shopping at a store? I would point at items or ask someone else to speak for me.

Wherever I went, my mind was filled with fear: "What if I stammer? What if people laugh? What if I can't complete my sentence?" But the truth is this: It's better to speak with a stammer than to stay silent out of fear.

MY OTHER STRENGTHS

While speaking was a constant struggle, there were a few things that came to me effortlessly.

And fortunately, my friends never saw me as "just a stammerer." They saw me as someone smart.

* Coding – While I hesitated to speak, my fingers danced confidently across the keyboard. I could solve problems, write code, and create things with ease.

* Cricket & Kabaddi – On the field, my stammer didn't matter. My actions spoke louder than my words.

* Team activities and fun games – During these games, I felt free through laughter and group interactions. No one cared about how I spoke—they only cared about how I played, contributed, and made the most of the moment.

These small victories motivated me and pushed me forward. They reminded me that my speech problem wasn't all that I was. Yes, I had battles within me—but I also had strengths. By the time I completed my college degree, I had learned a powerful lesson: Running away solves nothing. Facing it is the next step to success. Slowly, I began to free myself from the silence and continued my journey.

THE JOB HUNT

A Series of Failures – Success in Tests, Failures in Interviews

After finishing engineering, I entered the job market—a world whole of anxiety and excitement. On the one hand, I was hopeful—I easily cleared many written tests and coding rounds.

My technical skills were strong. But the moment I reached the next level, I failed—interviews that involved group discussions and communication.

I still vividly remember my first job interview. I entered the room, nervous but hopeful. But the moment I was asked to introduce myself, my voice froze. Words came out broken.

I could see the interviewer's patience fading. By the end of that round, I already knew the result: Rejected.

And that became the norm.

* Round 1: Aptitude & Coding—Pass.

* Round 2: Technical Discussion—Fail.

This kept happening—again and again.

50 INTERVIEWS. 50 REJECTIONS

By the time I reached my 50th interview, my self-confidence had hit rock bottom. I had studied so hard. Practiced coding day and night. But in every interview room, my biggest enemy wasn't the interviewer—it was my voice.

With every rejection, my doubts grew stronger:

* *"Maybe I'm just not fit for a corporate job."*

* *"Maybe I'll never recover from this stammer."*

* *"What's the point of trying when I already know the outcome?"*

While I was stuck in this painful cycle of rejection, I watched as all my friends started getting jobs one by one. And just when I hit my lowest point—Something happened.

THE MOMENT I ALMOST GAVE UP JOB HUNTING

After failing in so many interviews, my confidence was utterly shattered.

I began thinking: "Maybe software jobs aren't meant for me."

"Perhaps I should just accept whatever job comes my way." I stopped dreaming about my dream job and started attending interviews, thinking: "It doesn't matter what the job is—even if it has nothing to do with what I studied, I'll take it."

Surprisingly, I began receiving numerous job offers. One day, I was finally ready to join one of them. At that point, I just wanted to escape the never-ending cycle of rejection. Seeking my uncle's approval, I informed him about the job. But instead, he said something that changed my life:

"It's been only four months since you completed engineering. Why are you in such a hurry?

If you take a job in a field you didn't study for, just for the money, you'll regret it later. Give yourself one more year to try. Then decide where you want to go."

That hit me hard. He was right. I wasn't taking the job because I wanted to—I was taking it because I was exhausted from repeated failures. At that moment, I realised that not trying is a failure.

THE INTERVIEW THAT CHANGED EVERYTHING

One day, I received another interview call. However, by then, I had lost all enthusiasm. I told myself, "Even if I attend, I'll fail like always." So why bother?" I almost decided not to go. But at the last minute, I convinced myself: "Let's go just for the experience. I have nothing to lose." I easily cleared the first round (aptitude & coding) as usual.

A TEMPLE VISIT & A STRANGE FEELING

There was a long wait before the next round, so I visited a nearby temple instead of just sitting idle. I didn't pray for a job. I just sat there quietly, trying to calm my mind. And then, something strange happened. It was as if someone had whispered to me. A sudden thought entered my mind:

"You will get this job. This is your dream job. Believe in yourself."

I kept hearing that voice inside me. I felt a renewed sense of confidence for the first time in a long time. Someone or something guided me back to the path whenever I hit rock bottom.

Whether it was the friends who helped me during college, my uncle who encouraged me to try again, or this inner voice at the temple before the dream job interview, there was always a force, a light, showing me the way forward.

That moment gave me new energy. Instead of running away, I decided to fight for the career I truly wanted. And that's when everything began to change. With renewed determination, I returned to the job hunt—this time with a new mindset and strength.

THE FINAL INTERVIEW – STRUGGLE & SURPRISE

It turned out to be the most extended interview of my life. Finally, they said: "You are selected." I couldn't believe it. *"Why did they select me?"* I was so shocked I asked them directly: *"I struggled to speak... still, how did I get selected?"*

The company had only 50 employees at the time. Their answer completely changed how I saw myself: "We see you are skilled in using technology. We believe in your abilities. Once you start speaking more, your stammer will reduce over time."

That moment made me realise my true strength. For all those years, I had rejected myself before anyone else could. I thought no company would hire me because of my speech issue.

But this one company looked beyond it and saw my intellect and ability.

They didn't care how I spoke. They cared about what I knew and what I could do. That day, I learned a major life lesson:

Never count yourself out before giving it a try. You never know who's ready to believe in you."

That job wasn't just my first job but the beginning of my transformation. Yes, I still stammered and struggled in conversations. But for the first time, I didn't let my stammer hold me back.

Why shouldn't I believe in myself if someone else could believe in me? They didn't select me for how I spoke—They selected me because I knew my job. That job wasn't just a job—It was a turning point.

From that moment on, I stopped seeing myself as a failure. Even with flaws, I began to see myself as capable of rising.

RECOGNISED – BUT STILL NOT HEARD

My career started well. I performed technically at a high level and received several recognitions for my work. My problem-solving ability, coding skills, and project contributions were all praised. But one area still haunted me—presentations and discussions.

Whenever there was a group discussion, I would only speak when someone directly asked me a question. I never volunteered to speak. During technical debates, I hesitated, fearing my speech would make me look weak. For some time, I managed to avoid it. But one incident hit me deeply.

MY WORK – SOMEONE ELSE'S VOICE

After months of hard work, my manager called me one day: "You've done a great job technically. But because you struggle with presentations and answering questions, I want you to train someone else to present on your behalf."

Yes, he was right. The work was mine, but someone else would showcase it. That felt like a stab to the heart. It wasn't that I was being unrecognised or unappreciated by others. But I finally realised—my stammer was affecting my career growth.

If I didn't take action now, I would always stay behind, never moving forward. That was the moment I made a decision: No more running. It was time to fix this.

THE SEARCH FOR TREATMENT

I began looking for ways to cure my stammer. In Chennai, I searched for speech therapy centres, but I am still hoping for a solution. But every option I found came with its problems:

* Some were very expensive

* Some were too far away

* Some felt more like a business than a genuine effort to help

CHENNAI STAMMERING CARE CENTRE – A NEW HOPE

While searching online, I discovered the Chennai Stammering Care Centre. One unique detail caught my attention: It was run by a person who stammered himself. That felt different. Most stammering therapy centres are run by doctors, speech therapists, or specialists.

But this one? It was started by someone who had experienced stammering firsthand.

That's precisely what I had been searching for. My gut told me this was the right place. "Because this person will truly understand what I'm going through." So, I decided to meet him.

MEETING MR. MANIMARAN – A SURPRISING FIRST IMPRESSION

When I met Mr. Manimaran, something unexpected happened. While talking, he stammered, too, which confused me for a moment. "If he still stammers, how can he help me get cured?"

But then, he said something that completely changed my perspective: "I've learned to manage my stammer. I can teach you how to do the same." And the next surprise? All the training was completely free. I had nothing to lose.

So, I took a deep breath and said, "Okay... let's try this too." What happened next would become the turning point of my life.

A NEW PERSPECTIVE ON STAMMERING

Before meeting Mr. Manimaran, I thought he would give me techniques, tricks, or medicines to cure my stammer. Instead, he handed me a book and began explaining, stammering from an entirely new angle.

His approach wasn't about curing stammering but understanding and managing it.

His five core principles were simple but powerful:

1. Acceptance – Stop running away. Accept that you stammer. It's far better than hiding.

2. Awareness – Observe and understand *when* and *how* your stammer happens.

3. Friendship with Your Stammer – Don't Hate It. The more you fight it, the worse it gets. The moment you accept it, it loses its control over you.

4. Speak, Speak, speak – Avoiding speech makes stammering worse. Don't speak less—say more.

5. Consistent Practice – There's no overnight cure. Only daily practice leads to slow and steady progress.

These points seemed simple—But it took me 10 years to truly understand them.

WEEKLY MEETINGS – A SELF-HELP GROUP

Mr. Manimaran held weekly meetings for people like me. Every Sunday, about 10 of us would gather at his apartment in Kottur, Chennai. I attended my first session with scepticism. "What difference will this make?" I thought. But then... something magical happened. Fear Slowly Fades. In the early days, whenever I spoke, the same old fear returned:

* My heart would pound

* My throat would tighten

* My words would get stuck

But week after week, something began to change. I realised—I was no longer alone. I wasn't standing in front of a group that judged me—I was practicing in front of people just like me.

For the first time, I felt comfortable speaking. And the more I spoke, the more my fear faded.

A TURNING POINT – INSPIRED BY SURYA & YUVARAJ

Mr. Manimaran recommended speech exercises. At first, I didn't take them seriously. "Will this even work?" I wondered. But then I saw two friends—Surya and Yuvaraj—

Improve dramatically through those exercises. When they first joined, their stammering was as severe as mine. But after months of consistent practice, they began speaking fluently. Watching their transformation amazed me.

"If they can do it, why can't I?"

That became my turning point. I committed to doing daily speech exercises, and I practiced every day for the next six months. The results? Unbelievable.

* My speech improved by 80%

* My confidence soared to new heights

STAMMERING WORKSHOPS

Whether or not I always followed my daily practice perfectly, there were two things I never missed: the stammering workshops organised for people like me.

Two main reasons:

1. I felt light and joyful during those days, freely talking and interacting with others who shared my interests.

2. Most importantly, Mr. Manimaran often put me in charge of organising the workshops. As a result, I had more opportunities to speak on the mic than anyone else.

Over time, this not only improved my public speaking. But also drastically reduced my fear of speaking on stage.

A SMALL VICTORY THAT FELT LIKE A MIRACLE

One day, something happened—something that might seem ordinary to others. But to me, it was life-changing. For the first time, I bought a bus ticket alone. I ordered food at a restaurant— without a second thought. To someone who speaks fluently, this is nothing. But for me—this was everything.

For 27 years, I lived in fear of speaking. That day, I felt free for the very first time. I was flying. No, I wasn't speaking perfectly, but I was experiencing a new happiness I'd never felt before. That was the start of my transformation. For the first time, I had proof that change was possible. I didn't have to live forever in the shadow of my stammer.

A HARSH REMINDER

I was flying high with excitement. It felt like I had finally conquered my stammer. And then... it came back. After stopping my speech practice for a few months, I slowly began to stammer again. At first, I ignored it. "Maybe it's just a bad day," I thought. But as days passed, I realised —It wasn't just a bad day. It was a bad habit.

That's when Mr. Manimaran echoed: "Don't stop speech practice in the middle." Do it for at least a year." I had to learn that lesson the hard way. So, I restarted my practice, but this time, I did it with faith, belief, and full commitment.

Onsite Opportunity – A New Challenge Just as I got back on track, life threw a new challenge at me —I received an onsite job opportunity. It was a significant milestone—something I had always dreamed of. But along with excitement came fear:

* I had never travelled outside Tamil Nadu alone.

* I had never stayed away from home for more than a day.

* I had never been to another country.

I hesitated. "Can I do this?" In uncertain moments like this, I did what I always did —

I called Mr. Manimaran. His words were simple but powerful:

"You've come this far. Why doubt yourself now? Go. Experience life."

That one sentence was enough. I decided to leap.

A JOURNEY TO SOUTH AFRICA

For the first time in my life, I stepped out of Tamil Nadu on my own. I was going to live alone in a foreign country. I boarded a flight to South Africa, not knowing what to expect. Those six months changed me completely.

Finding Myself Living alone in another country taught me things. No classroom, no book, no training ever could. For the first time, I truly understood who Vinoth is —

And what he is capable of.

* I handled work challenges independently and confidently

* I managed everyday life without relying on anyone

* I adapted to a new culture, new people, and a completely different way of life

I wasn't just surviving during those six months—I was thriving. The same person who once hesitated to buy a ticket or order food? He no longer existed.

I had reinvented myself entirely —With complete confidence and belief that I could do anything. That international experience became the second central turning point of my life.

1.   First—overcoming stammering.

2.   Second—overcoming self-doubt.

A DREAM COME TRUE

After six months in South Africa, I returned to India with a new mindset. When I started looking for new opportunities this time, I faced rejection again. But I knew for the first time in my life: It wasn't because of my stammer. For years, every rejection shattered my confidence. But this time, I saw rejections as just another step in the journey. And eventually, I reached the place I had only dreamed of. From that point on, everything in my life started moving positively.

FROM A STRUGGLING STUDENT TO A TECH LEADER

Today, with over 10 years of experience. I lead a team of 20 technical professionals. Yes—*me*—the same person who once couldn't say his name without stammering.

I am the same person who avoided stages, interviews, and debates. Now, I guide others on my team and lead with confidence.

And this isn't just about career growth —It's about finally becoming the person I was always meant to be.

A SPECIAL THANK YOU

Much of my success is owed to Mr. Manimaran. He didn't just teach me how to overcome stammering —He helped me discover who I am. Once you realise your true potential, nothing can stop you. At the end of the day —The only thing standing between you and success is your self-doubt. Remove that...And the world is yours.

PERSONAL LIFE

I got married in 2018. It brought me great joy when Mr. Manimaran and his wife attended my wedding. My wife is a homemaker. Even when I met her family, I had already been transparent about my stammering. It had significantly improved, so they assumed I was completely cured.

We now have a 5-year-old son. At the age of 2, he spoke clearly. After six months, he began to stammer slightly. But once he started school, his speech improved. Even now, he occasionally stammers—but he's actively trying to improve.

FINAL MESSAGE: THE POWER OF PERSISTENCE

Looking back, if I could tell young people one thing, it would be this: "Keep going. Keep going, no matter how hard it gets or how often you fail." For years, I believed my stammer was a curse that would always hold me back.

But the truth is, it never held me back. What held me back were my fears, self-doubt, and hesitation. My entire life changed when I stopped running from my stammer and chose to accept it.

TO EVERYONE STRUGGLING WITH STAMMERING (OR ANYTHING ELSE)

* You are more capable than you think.

* Your failures do not define you—your persistence does.

* Every challenge you overcome will make you stronger.

It took me years to understand this, but everything started to fall into place once I did. Now, as I lead a team, face challenges, and continue to grow, one thing is sure: The best version of Vinoth isn't somewhere in the future. He's always been within me. I just needed to believe in him.

And so do you. Believe in yourself. This journey doesn't end here—it never ends. But today, I move forward with no fear and complete confidence, which makes all the difference.

K. Vinoth Kumar – Chennai - Tamil Nadu

Email: sendamailtovinoth@gmail.com

10

SUPER HERO

His name is Surya. His father was a daily wage labourer who passed away three years ago. His mother is a homemaker. Surya is the eldest in the family. He has two younger sisters and one younger brother. Surya's family is impoverished. Specifically, until a few years ago, they could only afford two meals a day. His parents strongly desire to provide a good education for Surya. Their greatest wish is for him to get a government job somehow.

Surya studied in a government-aided school. While in school, he was also interested in sports. He excelled particularly in cricket and kabaddi. He was a brilliant student, too. From grades 1 to 12, he consistently scored high marks. In 8th grade, he secured the first rank in the school; in 10th, he was second; and in 12th, he again secured the first rank.

Even though he was an outstanding student, he could not shine in other artistic fields. He strongly desired to participate in and win cultural and literary competitions held in schools. He loved public speaking and wanted everyone to pay attention to his speech. But the harsh truth was that he couldn't do it. The reason was his stammering problem, which he had since childhood. This stammering caused him significant mental stress.

In those early days, he tried many things as far as his understanding could take him. He tried repeatedly placing pebbles in his mouth while speaking and also cleaning his tongue. When he thinks about those efforts now, he finds them amusing. He even visited a doctor with his father. But the doctor said, "This will go away with time," and sent him back. No matter how much he tried, he couldn't speak fluently.

As a result, he often became the subject of his friends' mockery. Teachers would ask Surya to stand up and read from the textbook in the early stages. But when he began stammering while reading, they would ask him to sit down. The same happened in every class. All the other students in the class would read fluently. Surya would look at them longingly, thinking, "Why can't I read like them?" The only sentence he regularly spoke in class was "Present, Sir" during attendance.

Once, Surya got the opportunity to speak through the school's microphone. He was in the 6th grade at the time. He had to speak at 9:30 in the morning. Surya practised his speech many times and stood in front of the microphone. But only air came out of his mouth—no words. From that day until he finished school, he was never invited to speak on the microphone again. That incident affected him deeply. Believing that stammerers would have to live their entire lives stammering. Surya somehow completed his schooling.

All his teachers used to say, "Surya is an excellent student, but he just can't speak properly." He faced many humiliating public experiences. He couldn't even buy a bus ticket. If his mother sent him to the store to buy some items, he couldn't bring them back correctly.

Once, when Surya requested leave from his teacher and had to explain why, he stammered a lot. Thinking his time was wasted, the teacher scolded Surya and sent him away. This deeply hurt Surya. As a result, he didn't take leave the next day either.

Although Surya experienced many painful situations due to stammering, there were also some amusing incidents occasionally. During his school days, he couldn't pronounce the name of his stop, *Kadachanenthal*, while buying a bus ticket. So, he would always ask for a ticket to the next stop, *S.R. Patti*, and get down at *Kadachanenthal*. But once, the bus didn't stop at his actual stop. Following the ticket, the new conductor let him off at S.R. Patti, which was farther. Surya had no choice but to walk two kilometres back to his village.

He had a small circle of friends with whom he could speak comfortably. One day, his school life came to an end. He passed his 12th grade with excellent marks and was the top student in his school. Because of his high scores, he was allotted a seat in the Mechanical Engineering stream at the College of Engineering, Guindy (CEG), under Anna University—one of the top-ranked engineering colleges in India. His parents, friends, and teachers were all thrilled by his achievement. But Surya couldn't share in their happiness. His mind was burdened by one thought—*his stammering*. He began to worry about how he would manage it in college.

He had no idea how to undergo training or therapy to fix his stammering. More painfully, no one he could even talk to about it. With a heavy heart, he began his college life. Another reason for his emotional strain was that he had never been away from his parents until then.

Surya was accompanied by his mother, father, and sister on the first day of college. It was announced that Dr. A.P.J. Abdul Kalam Sir would visit the college that day, so everyone was busy preparing. Surya felt like a *frog in a well* thrown into the sea—completely lost and overwhelmed.

At the hostel, his father, like a concerned parent, asked the hostel warden questions like someone doing it for a small child. But the warden brushed him off, saying, "We'll take care of everything! You can leave peacefully." Even then, only one thought kept running through Surya's mind: "What if I have to ask the warden for something tomorrow? How will I talk to him? Should I tell him in advance that I stammer?"

Time passed, and eventually, his parents left him at the hostel and returned home.

Surya looked for a friend who would match his mindset. He found one—Mani, a fellow hostel student from the Kallakurichi district. Like Surya, he, too, was a *frog in the well.* The two quickly became good friends. Surya never told Mani about his past struggles with stammering in school. He didn't want his college life to be affected the same way. So, from the first year of college, Surya started trying to recover from his stammering. His first step was—to talk with everyone.

But his mistake was that he never truly accepted his stammering. He spoke only in safe environments and avoided difficult situations.

Even though Surya could speak well in comfortable situations and converse fluently with certain friends, a false belief formed in his mind—*"I can speak well."* But he didn't realise then that this was not how to overcome stammering.

The truth is Surya didn't face many difficult situations in college. The only challenging situation he encountered regularly was during attendance. In school, attendance was taken just once a day. But in college, it had to be given in every class. Surya was a top-performing student in school, so he easily stood out. But in college, things were different.

As mentioned earlier, Surya had joined one of the top colleges in India. Most students there were fluent in English and skilled with computers. On the other hand, Surya studied in a government-aided Tamil-medium school. So, he couldn't shine like those students. Still, he scored over 80% in every semester through sheer effort. He was like one star in college among the countless stars in the sky.

Eventually, he even found a way to manage the stress of answering attendance. While that may seem like a positive thing, in truth, Surya had only expanded his comfort zone a little. He did not face the same challenging situations in college that he had faced in school.

Time went by, and the third year of college came to an end. In March 2014, Surya went to a reputed engineering college in Chennai to attend a job recruitment drive conducted by the Indian Army. Final-year engineering students were eligible to participate. If selected, one could join the Indian Military as an engineer.

The recruitment had two stages—Group Discussion (GD) and Interview.

Surya and a close friend went together. In Surya's mind, he believed, *"I speak well with my friends; I can easily clear this."* But that day didn't go the way he expected.

He was called for the group discussion round with his friend and students from other colleges. There were eight participants in the group. The group discussion began, and one by one, everyone started speaking. Everyone was expected to participate.

When it was Surya's turn—not a single word came out of his mouth. Just like in 6th grade, when he stood silently in front of the microphone, the same thing happened again. His friend spoke well that day.

Surya was shocked. "I speak well with friends, and I even manage classroom attendance. How *could I not speak a single word today?"*

That's when it finally hit him—*"I didn't deceive my stammering; it deceived me!"* The truth was, he had never accepted his stammering openly.

When Surya later asked his friend about the incident, the friend said, "You only stammer occasionally. But today, you didn't say even one word. Why?"

That moment gave Surya clarity—*If I want to move forward in life, I must be able to speak fluently in public.*

Surya shared everything with his father, who comforted him. That night, Surya couldn't sleep. He kept thinking about how to speak better, so he began searching the internet.

A week later, he found a TISA—The Chennai Chapter link that included Mr. Manimaran's phone number. Nervously and hesitantly, Surya called him.

Mr Manimaran kindly invited Surya to meet in person. At that time, Manimaran ran the Chennai Stammering Care Center for free in his apartment building in Kottur.

The centre was about 2 km away from Surya's college.

Surya borrowed his friend's bicycle and went there. But it wasn't just about stepping out of college—it felt like stepping out of a well and into the ocean.

Surya went to Mr. Manimaran's office in Kottur. Only after reaching there did, he realise it wasn't an office—it was Mr. Manimaran's home. He had converted his home into a centre because he didn't want others to suffer from stammering the way he had. Surya met Mr. Manimaran there, and that meeting became a turning point in his life.

Mr. Manimaran clearly explained to Surya what stammering is, how to overcome it, how speech practice works, and how long it should be done. Only then did Surya genuinely begin to understand stammering.

From that day onward, he would take his friend's bicycle to the centre daily. When his friends asked where he was going, Surya said nothing. He thought he would tell them later, after he improved his speech. He sincerely followed all the practice techniques that Mr. Manimaran taught.

The emotional void he had felt throughout school and college, of not having anyone to guide him in overcoming his stammer, was now filled through Mr. Manimaran. Without missing even a single day, Surya went to the centre. He practiced consistently, performing both speech and breathing exercises with complete dedication.

Many others regularly came to the centre, including Mr Yuvaraj, Mr Gnanasekaran, Mr Vinoth, Mr Ganesh, and Mr Karunya Moorthy—stammerers like Surya. He would join the group daily and participate in speech and group practice sessions.

Initially, he couldn't speak fluently during group sessions. But the others encouraged him and bonded with him warmly. Eventually, he began speaking confidently in group practices, improving his speech significantly. Surya could feel this improvement. He slowly started recording himself speaking in small public places. He had pushed his boundaries to the next level.

His final year of college arrived—the most crucial year. That year, he had to complete a major project. Surya was appointed project team leader for both semesters and earned good marks for the project work. However, deep down, he still hadn't entirely emotionally accepted his stammer, which bothered him.

He asked Mr. Manimaran about this lingering discomfort. Manimaran replied, "Only when you truly accept your stammering from the heart will you be able to speak well." From that day onward, Surya started accepting his stammer. He practiced with even greater effort—from March 2014 to May 2015, he practiced daily. As a result, he achieved remarkable fluency in his speech.

In the final semester of college, he fearlessly attended all campus interviews. He was offered jobs at Infosys and Murugappa Motors. Later, he also attended an interview at Bharat Petroleum, a government-owned oil company in Mumbai. He confidently cleared both rounds of group discussion and received the offer for that job as well (which is why he didn't join Infosys or Murugappa Motors). However, he couldn't take up the Bharat Petroleum job for other reasons.

Still, Surya did not lose heart. He wanted to get a government job, his parents' dream. He started preparing for bank exams and succeeded. In 2017, he joined a reputed government rural bank as an Assistant Officer. Through his hard work and dedication, he was later promoted to Manager.

His long-standing dream was to speak on stage. Surya didn't just get on one stage—he spoke on many and even recorded his speeches. He speaks more fluently in the bank where he works than even those considered great speakers.

Surya got married in April 2021. By then, he had almost wholly overcome his stammering and could speak fluently. So, he did not need to even mention to his future wife that he used to stammer. Today, they have a 2-year-old son.

As his parents wished, Surya is now well-settled in a government job. But even now, his stammer walks with him. He has entirely accepted it and is living a happy life.

Here is Surya's advice to others who stammer, in his own words:

"I may not be old enough to give advice, but I'm sharing this so that others don't go through the same pain I did. Overcoming stammering is tough—but not impossible. You must follow the proper practices diligently.

Because of stammering, we face many challenges in life. So, the first step is to accept that you stammer. Say it out loud and be open about it—that itself is half the cure. No matter how busy your daily life is, you must dedicate at least one hour daily to speech therapy.

Do the practices sincerely and with full faith. Also, be sure to participate in group meetings.

If we follow these consistently, we can all overcome stammering with ease.

Let's stay hopeful. Let's overcome stammering.

I don't say I am entirely cured of stammering, but I have overcome most of it and now manage it well. Thanks to the speech practices I followed, I started speaking clearly and fluently.

Now that I speak well, I no longer need to practice those daily. However, I still actively participate in all group meetings. Even today, I remain a good example and inspiration to the Tamil Super Speakers (TSS) group members."

This story is dedicated to my Mentor, Mr. Manimaran Sir.

B. Surya – Madurai - Tamil Nadu

Email: surya15293@gmail.com

11

FOUR DIGITS TO SIX DIGITS

P. Yuvaraj was born in 1990 into a lower-middle-class family in Perambur, Chennai. His father worked in a private company for a low salary, and his mother was a homemaker. Yuvaraj has one younger sister. From the time he began speaking, Yuvaraj had a stammer. No one else in his family had such a speech difficulty.

Yuvaraj was a bright student in school. From Grades 1 to 5, he always secured first rank. From Grades 6 to 12, he consistently ranked between 6th and 7th. He was never mocked or teased by teachers or classmates. When teachers asked students to read from textbooks aloud, Yuvaraj was also asked to participate, unlike many teachers who avoid asking students with speech issues.

After completing school, Yuvaraj pursued a B.E. in Computer Science Engineering (2007–2011) at a private engineering college in Veppampattu, near Thiruvallur. In 2010, he participated in a symposium at Sriram Engineering College, where he and his team presented a skit in front of 2,000 people and won third prize. Yuvaraj played a key role in that team.

All student groups had to present their final-year projects to professors and lecturers during their final year. Yuvaraj's teammates, although fluent speakers, asked him to present in his group of three. Despite his stammer, Yuvaraj delivered the presentation confidently and helped his team earn good marks.

Apart from struggling slightly during attendance roll calls in school and college, Yuvaraj didn't face many issues. However, during campus interviews, he was only offered a call centre job, which he declined because he wanted to pursue a career in software development, given his strong academic performance.

After graduating, Yuvaraj worked small jobs while preparing for bank and central government exams. For two years, he took several competitive exams. Though he often came close to the cut-off marks, he could not clear them.

Over the next four years, he worked in various jobs. Realising that his speech disorder was the main obstacle to landing a good job, he decided to find a solution.

While searching online, Yuvaraj found Mr. Manimaran's phone number. He contacted him and visited the Chennai Stammering Care Centre (CSCC) in Kottur in May 2014. Mr. Manimaran explained stammering, how to practice speech, and how openly accepting one's stammer helps reduce fear. He also demonstrated how to practice effectively.

Yuvaraj began attending weekly Self Help Group (SHG) meetings at CSCC but did not practice for the first two months. Then came Friendship Day, on a Sunday, during an SHG meeting attended by over 10 people. That day, Yuvaraj gave a fantastic speech in front of everyone. That speech became a turning point, igniting a spark within him.

Yuvaraj was working at a small company at the time. Every day after work, he would reach CSCC by 6 PM. He would meet Surya, a student from nearby Guindy Engineering College. Both of them would practice speech therapy in separate rooms from 6 to 7 PM. From 7 to 8 PM, they would simulate classroom teaching on a whiteboard. Mr. Manimaran and Mr. Ganesh were always present to guide them.

Yuvaraj practiced continuously for a year. Whenever he could, he visited CSCC and spoke on various topics. Mr. Gnanasekar was another frequent visitor, and one of his classes, "Little Me—Big Me," deeply resonated with Yuvaraj.

He actively participated in all early TISA workshops. Notably, in May 2018, Agniraj came from Madurai to Chennai to attend a workshop, and Yuvaraj was one of the key organisers. In every workshop he attended, Yuvaraj conducted a session on "Little Me – Big Me."

LITTLE ME – BIG ME: A POWERFUL INSIGHT

Yuvaraj teaches that people who stammer should always think of themselves as the "Big Me" whenever they can speak. That mindset builds confidence. However, to feel like the "Big Me," one must possess a broad knowledge base. You won't feel like the Big Me if you are ignorant, even if you speak fluently.

Before understanding "Little Me – Big Me," many people who stammer speak fluently at home or with close friends. That's because they're in a comfort zone, and everyone knows their stammer. There's no pressure to speak fluently. But in public or with superiors, that comfort disappears—and that's when the Little Me – Big Me concept becomes invaluable.

YUVARAJ EXPLAINS (IN HIS OWN WORDS)

Little Me – Whenever I feel small or inferior, I stammer. For example, when I speak with my manager and feel he is superior, I become anxious and stammer. That self-doubt and power imbalance increase my stammer.

Big Me – The exact opposite of Little Me. When I view myself as equal or empowered, I do not stammer. I speak fluently with a positive mindset and a strong belief in my competence. Confidence flows naturally.

CAREER BREAKTHROUGHS

After a year of regular speech practice, Yuvaraj began attending interviews at top companies. He finally landed a job at one of India's top three IT companies—a dream for many. He worked there for five years, mastering job-related tasks and improving his English fluency.

Once, during a weekly status review call, Yuvaraj had to present on behalf of his project team. The 20-minute presentation included noticeable stammering, and both his Vice President and Manager criticised him afterwards. Though embarrassed, he took it as a challenge. Four months later, he delivered a fluent and impressive presentation to the same group and was well received.

While at that company, he learned many software and project management techniques. After five years, he moved to another top-tier IT company as a Deputy Project Manager. He led over 40 employees with confidence and handled day-to-day interactions with international clients. He served in this role for two years.

Today, Yuvaraj works as a project manager at a multinational IT company headquartered in Canada, drawing a six-figure salary.

MESSAGE TO THE YOUTH

Yuvaraj strongly advises:

"Practice speech therapy without fail. In today's world, communication is everything. No matter how intelligent you are, securing a position at a top company is challenging if you can't speak fluently. Just follow the techniques from the TSS group for one year— you'll speak well and land a great job with a good salary."

Yuvaraj got married in 2022. His wife, a former college lecturer, is now a homemaker. They have a 2-year-old son.

He has pledged to financially support the education of individuals who stammer and also plans to offer free training in soft skills and IT skills to help other stammerers succeed.

P. Yuvaraj – Chennai – Tamil Nadu

Email: yuvarajponnuswamy17@gmail.com

12

THE VICTORIOUS STRUGGLE AGAINST STAMMERING

I, Meganathan, was born in 1976 in the small town of Mettur, Tamil Nadu, and grew up there. I have one brother and one sister. My father worked as a contract labourer for the Tamil Nadu Electricity Board (TNEB) for almost ten years before getting a permanent position. To support our five-member family, he took up various part-time jobs. These included working as a security guard at a shop, a cook, and a labourer at another place. My mother was a homemaker.

We lived in a hut for nearly five years, which used to leak during the rainy season. My parents were uneducated, so they enrolled me in a government school in Mettur.

During school vacations (quarterly, half-yearly, and annual), I used to work to help my father. On some days, I sold lottery tickets under the hot sun. During my school and college days, I worked in bookshops, hotels, oil mills, and lodges whenever I could.

From a young age, I realised I had a stammering problem. No one else in my family had this issue. I couldn't speak fluently without stammering. At school and college, among friends and relatives, I was known as "the stammering boy." Because of that label, I often felt very low. I avoided cultural events and never stepped on stage until my post-graduation years.

Whenever I tried to speak at school, the other children mocked me. I would often return home crying. Whenever I felt upset, my father would take me to MBBS doctors or ENT specialists. Doctors would assure us that I would eventually speak well, but nothing worked.

Some relatives suggested speaking with a pebble in the mouth. I tried that, too, but it didn't help. The stammering problem made me an introvert. I didn't socialise much, which affected my self-esteem.

Despite financial struggles and my stammering issue, I excelled academically. I studied in the Tamil medium up to the 12th grade in a government school, passing with good marks, and stood second in English despite competition from students in English-medium schools. I was one of the state rank holders in Accountancy and scored 200 out of 200 on the final exam. My photo was published in many newspapers, but I couldn't afford a copy. The next day, I visited a local saloon and inquired about the previous day's newspaper. I still have some of those clippings.

My high scores made me admitted to Sacred Heart College in Tirupattur for undergraduate studies. During college, my stammering problem was so severe that I couldn't even say my roll number during attendance. Each student had to call out their number. When my turn came, I would hesitate and pause for a long time. My professor often scolded me, which embarrassed me in every class. Fortunately, one of my classmates noticed this and started calling my roll number on my behalf. That was a massive relief for me.

Because of my stammering, I avoided speaking in public and never participated in extracurricular activities. The ridicule

I faced deeply affected my mental and emotional well-being. During college, I tried different remedies like meditation, but nothing worked.

Since I studied in Tamil medium at school, adapting to the English language in college was challenging. Even so, I completed my degree with 70% marks.

Later, I pursued a master's degree in Human Resources (HR). At that time, I didn't realise how essential communication skills were required for a successful career in HR. I struggled to speak under pressure during internships, summer training, and placements. Although a good student, I couldn't perform well in Viva exams. These exams required me to explain my field experience and the lessons I learned. I would tremble and stammer, which affected my marks. My overall scores would be excellent in all subjects, except Viva. The low Viva score affected my total marks.

As part of my internship, I worked in the HR department at TITAN. When alone, I struggled to speak fluently on the phone, so I hesitated even to pick up the landline. As a result, I avoided answering calls.

Despite these challenges, I graduated in 1998, placing third in my batch. When I started job hunting, I was referred to a recruitment consultant. When I met him, he asked me to introduce myself. I couldn't speak and was very nervous. After seeing my stammer, he said, "With this handicap, it's hard for you to get a job in HR." He emphasised that communication skills were vital in HR.

I felt deeply discouraged. I almost gave up on my dream of working in HR. However, by chance, I landed a job at a pharmaceutical company. Since I couldn't speak well, I decided that hard work would be my path to success. I arrived on time, stayed late, and worked diligently. That approach paid off. People began to notice my dedication, and I earned a good reputation at work. This helped me gain respect, grow in my career, and build self-confidence. I started earning money, and my friends and relatives began to respect me. Some even looked up to me as a role model.

Gradually, I developed managerial skills like presentation and communication. I moved to more prominent corporate organisations from the pharmaceutical company and earned recognition in the HR field. These achievements helped me manage my stammering. I can proudly say that I have almost completely overcome it.

I joined Toastmasters International; a nonprofit organisation that helps people improve their public speaking skills. It further strengthened my communication skills.

In 2018, I was invited to speak at a Tamil Super Speakers workshop in Chennai for individuals with stammering. As I was from HR, I conducted a mock interview on stage with a few individuals who were stammerers. It impressed everyone.

Today, I'm pleased to share that I serve as a Deputy General Manager (DGM) in Human Resources at a primary public sector company in Maharashtra. No one at my workplace knew I had a stammering issue until I was 30. I've entirely overcome that challenge. My friends and relatives are happy for me. One of my relatives, who studies astrology, even took my life as a case study to see if there was any connection between my horoscope and this transformation.

I got married in 2001. It was a love marriage. My wife never mentioned my stammering. Falling in love increased my confidence and helped me manage the issue. If someone can love you despite your stammering, it boosts your self-confidence. That's what happened in my life.

I have two sons—my elder one is in the final year of engineering, and the younger one is in the 9th grade. Neither of them has any speech issues and are excellent speakers.

I don't believe HR would reject someone because of a speech issue. For training, teaching, or marketing jobs, fluency in speaking may be essential, as HR may prefer candidates who are good speakers. Otherwise, if you're technically strong and academically consistent, it won't be a problem.

I believe stammerers can improve if they keep practicing. Most face this problem during their youth and learn to manage it with time. I've never met anyone over 40 who still stammers severely, so time does help reduce it. It's not a disease—it's related to our mind. We need confidence. Joining a speaker club, such as Toastmasters, can be beneficial.

Meditation and yoga are also beneficial. They help keep us calm. Due to our stammering, we often speak quickly to finish sentences. It's better to speak slowly. Practicing a few techniques may help. We also know which words we tend to stammer on. For example, I struggle with pronouncing words like *Preethi* and *Kriti*. Notice that all these words have the second letter "r." So, I'm extra cautious while saying such words.

I am grateful to everyone who has helped and supported me. There is a science behind gratitude—it contributes to personal growth.

Although I can't pinpoint one exact reason for overcoming this issue, I'm sure that hard work played a significant role in my success.

N. Meganathan – Mumbai - Maharashtra

Email: meganathannarayanan@gmail.com

13

WAVES NEVER REST

Vallinayagam was born in 1980 into a modest middle-class family in Chennai. He has two younger sisters. Since both his parents discontinued their schooling midway, he grew up believing that *education alone could transform his life*. His early school days went by smoothly—until he began to stammer.

Once his stammering started, it drew teasing and ridicule from neighbours and friends. What began mildly worsened due to the reactions of those around him. He was the only one in his family who stammer; everyone else spoke fluently.

His stammering not only became a challenge, but it also became his *identity*. He was labelled *shy* and *introverted* and silently endured people's stares. Like many who stammer, Vallinayagam excelled in academics, and his talents were undeniable.

On his 7th-grade school annual day, he won first prizes in essay writing and drawing and second in handwriting—but he never entered the speech competition. He didn't dare to participate because of his stammer. Though it saddened him, he found comfort in his other achievements, telling himself, *"At least I'm winning in other areas."* This positive mindset led him forward and helped him get admission into a reputed college for the course of his choice.

COLLEGE YEARS – TRIUMPHS AND TRIALS

In college, Vallinayagam was known for his persistence and dedication. One of his lecturers was known to be a strict disciplinarian. On one occasion, the lecturer asked about an assignment. Vallinayagam explained that he had to attend another class the previous day and could not complete it. To everyone's surprise, the lecturer said, *"If Vallinayagam couldn't do it, no one else could,"* and forgave the entire class. That moment of trust and recognition filled him with pride and joy.

But in the next class, that trust was shattered. During roll call in a math class, Vallinayagam couldn't immediately respond "present" due to his stammering. Mistaking his hesitation for absence, the lecturer marked him absent. Vallinayagam later went to the lecturer's room and explained his speech issue and that he had attended the class. The lecturer, though reluctant, corrected the attendance. But his classmates whispered, *"Looks like Vallinayagam's dubbing friends aren't here today."* That remark deeply hurt him.

THE STRUGGLE FOR EMPLOYMENT

After graduation, Vallinayagam faced numerous challenges while job hunting. He passed aptitude and written tests but repeatedly failed in interviews and group discussions. Each rejection shook his confidence. One day, his close friend Venkatesh offered life-changing advice:

"You're very talented. Why waste time brooding? Focus on your strengths."

Taking that advice to heart, Vallinayagam focused on competitive exams. With little coaching or preparation, he cleared the NABARD and SBI bank exams in his first attempt. He chose NABARD and began his career as a Grade A Officer.

REBUILDING CONFIDENCE AND FINDING HIS VOICE

With renewed confidence, Vallinayagam didn't stop there. He continued to upskill and landed a job at the Centre for Development of Advanced Computing (CDAC) in Bangalore. He fully immersed himself in computer science and technology.

Encouraged by these successes, Vallinayagam set his sights on the private sector. But switching from government to private companies wasn't easy—his stammer remained a significant obstacle.

During this time, he discovered TISA (The Indian Stammering Association) online. Through TISA's Self-Help Group (SHG), he met inspiring people like Dr. Bhaskar, who held a PhD and shared the same philosophy as his friend Venkatesh: *"Focus on your strengths."*

He also learned valuable speech techniques from Mr. Manimaran, TISA's then-Tamil Nadu coordinator and now the TSS group's founder. Although he didn't practice speech exercises regularly, Vallinayagam consistently shared voice recordings in the group, which boosted his self-confidence. Eventually, he came to accept his stammer fully. Even if he stammers occasionally, it doesn't bother or frighten him.

TURNING POINT AND CAREER GROWTH

Fuelled by newfound hope, Vallinayagam doubled his efforts. Soon, he received five job offers simultaneously. He ultimately accepted his dream job in the IT sector. Around this time, he also read the book *"Strengths Finder," which further reinforced his belief that focusing on strengths can lead to unparalleled* success.

INSPIRING THE NEXT GENERATION

Today, Vallinayagam thrives in his dream job, earning well and living the life he once thought impossible. From a shy boy mocked for stammering, he has grown into a confident professional—his journey stands as a testament to courage and determination.

His wife is a homemaker. Before marriage, he had openly shared about his stammering. She accepted him fully and has always supported him in every way. They have a daughter in the 10th grade and a son in the 5th. The family now lives peacefully in Hyderabad.

HIS MESSAGE FOR OTHERS FACING SPEECH OR PERSONAL CHALLENGES

✽   *"Don't let your weakness overshadow your talent."*

✽   *"If you wait for the waves to settle, you'll never swim in the sea."*

Vallinayagam's story is not just about overcoming stammering. It celebrates the human spirit's power to overcome limitations, find strength in struggle, and achieve greatness.

P. Vallinayagam – Hyderabad - Telangana

Email: p.vallinayagam@gmail.com

14

A STRONG FOUNDATION IS REQUIRED TO BUILD A GOOD HOUSE

P. Poovarasan was born in 1994 in Washermenpet, North Chennai. He is the elder of two siblings. His family lived modestly—his father was a daily wage labourer, and his mother a homemaker. Until age three, Poovarasan lived in a joint family with his grandparents, uncle, and aunt. As a child, he was constantly scolded by everyone around him for no reason—even his mother was scolded. He was reprimanded for touching anything, warned about spirits in the bushes, and constantly frightened. These fears deeply impacted him, planting seeds of anxiety that lingered into adolescence.

Eventually, they moved out of the joint family into a separate home. As school age approached, he was enrolled in a local school in Washermenpet and studied there until Grade 5. He spoke fluently up to Grade 3. However, in Grade 4, he began stammering after regularly interacting with a stammering girl in his class. Whether it was imitation or influence, he doesn't know.

His parents didn't take it seriously. In 2004, when they tried to enrol him in another school, his mother asked him to read a lesson aloud for practice. He stammered heavily. Alarmed, she took him to Stanley Medical College Hospital, where a doctor prescribed tablets and told her he would outgrow it. But the stammer persisted.

He completed Grades 6 to 12 at a school in Royapuram. During attendance, he would quickly say whatever words came to mind, such as "Yes, Sir" or "Present, Sir." Thankfully, he was never teased by classmates. He loved maths, and teachers appreciated his knowledge of the subject. But when he stood up to answer a question, some teachers would ask him to sit down, assuming he couldn't speak clearly.

Once, he was the only one in class who knew the answer to a math problem. The teacher asked him to explain, but he couldn't get even a single word out. The teacher then asked him to solve it on the board—which he did perfectly. Still, he considered his inability to speak aloud as a major humiliation and stopped talking in class after that.

Despite these hurdles, he scored 1061/1200 in Grade 12. With such good marks, he secured a government quota seat at a reputable private engineering college near Chennai. Since most of his classmates were from other states, they didn't focus on his speech issue.

In his first year, he always sat in the front row—not out of enthusiasm, but because professors typically asked students to introduce themselves. By sitting in front, he could finish quickly and relax while others took their turn. If he sat in the back, the waiting would make him increasingly nervous.

In the second year, his stream was split, and he joined the Civil Engineering program. Now, his class was three times larger. Seating was arranged by height, so he ended up in the last row— meaning he would be the last to introduce himself. As his turn neared, his heart would pound. Introducing himself was an absolute nightmare. Only after he finished speaking would he feel like he had "come back to life."

He could speak well with family and close friends. However, if asked a question unexpectedly or if he had to speak loudly to strangers, he would stammer badly. He never went out alone; he always went with friends.

Once, his mother asked him to buy onions, tomatoes, and a coconut from a store. When he tried to speak to the shopkeeper, he couldn't utter a single word. The shopkeeper, understanding his struggle, gave him paper to write down the items. Poovarasan wrote them, got the items, went home, and burst into tears. His mother consoled him.

Ordering food at restaurants was also tricky. His favourite dish was chicken fried rice, but he couldn't say "Chicken" fluently. He would ask for "fried rice," hoping the server would list options. Once "chicken fried rice" was mentioned, he would repeat it. He also couldn't say "ten" clearly. So, if asked to buy 10 parottas, he would get 11 and say it was on purpose to avoid saying "ten." If his mother asked why, he would say, 'Because I want one extra, I bought 11.

Unlike many others with the same issue, Poovarasan did not stammer while talking to women. At his college, where talking to the opposite gender was discouraged, he was the first to break the barrier, connecting with female students via WhatsApp and Facebook to exchange notes and build friendships.

CAREER CHALLENGES AND TURNING POINTS

In his final year, placement interviews began. Poovarasan easily cleared the written exams but would often skip interviews due to fear. He graduated without getting placed.

Many of his friends got software jobs through campus placement. Some went abroad. Others pursued higher studies. Poovarasan remained jobless.

Determined to fix his stammer, he tried traditional techniques—reading aloud and putting pebbles in his mouth. In 2017, a school friend recommended that to try acupuncture. It came to light that such a clinic existed in Nungambakkam. Poovarasan's friend contacted the clinic and made an appointment with him. The next day, Poovarasan went there for treatment. The chief doctor at the clinic began treating him. He inserted many needles all over his body and then left. After about 45 minutes, another doctor came and removed all the needles.

Then, he looked at Poovarasan and asked what problem he had come for. Poovarasan explained his speech issue. In response, that doctor said that he, too, stammered and that speech problems could not be cured through acupuncture. He advised Poovarasan to undergo speech therapy and mentioned that a WhatsApp group for that purpose was active in Chennai and recommended that he join it. Just then, the chief doctor returned, and their conversation ended there.

That doctor quoted ₹10,000 for 10 sessions. But Poovarasan decided to pursue speech training instead.

At home, he searched online for the "Chennai stammering WhatsApp group" and found Mr Manimaran's number. Afraid to call, he messaged him on WhatsApp. Manimaran immediately replied and invited him to his home—which was just 2 km away.

Poovarasan learned that Manimaran was also a civil engineer and had retired as a Chief Engineer in a Tamil Nadu government department. Manimaran explained stammering, why acceptance is key, and how to practice speech. He taught Poovarasan a technique and asked him to practice it for one hour daily, then added him to the TSS (Tamil Super Speakers) WhatsApp group.

JOINING TSS AND REBUILDING CONFIDENCE

The TSS group had daily tasks. Members recorded how long they practiced daily and shared a 3-minute voice message on a given topic. Around 10 members gathered at a public place in Chennai every Sunday to discuss, share stories, and motivate one another. For Poovarasan, this group was a spark—it felt like *home*. He began practicing daily.

In March 2018, he fearlessly attended an interview at a civil engineering company. The employer did not notice his stammer—instead, he saw his confidence and skills and offered him the job.

He began as a trainee and, through hard work, progressed to supervisor, site engineer, and ultimately executive engineer. Despite his responsibilities, he was paid only ₹14,000 per month. In comparison, his friends earned ₹80,000 to ₹1 lakh.

He wanted to grow but was hesitant to start his own company due to a lack of family backing or resources. His father was a plumber, his mother a homemaker, and his brother was still studying. He didn't have well-off relatives to support him.

Still motivated by TSS mentors like Agnee Raj, he continued to push forward. Inspired by Alphonse, another stammerer who runs a successful photo studio with 10 staff, Poovarasan realised, *"If he can, why not me?"*

In January 2022, he launched his construction company, Urban Lion Homes. He spread the word through friends, relatives, Facebook, and Instagram.

Soon, he heard about an unfinished house in Madhavaram. With courage, he approached the owner and secured a contract. In three months, he completed the house, and that success brought him more projects.

Now, 30 people work for his company. He has built eight homes and is currently working on two more. He has begun constructing homes on clients' land and plans to purchase his land for apartments. He practices speech daily—it has been over

1,000 days of consistent training. He now speaks fluently; he doesn't fear it even when he stammers.

FINAL WORDS FROM POOVARASAN

"Only correct speech practice, acceptance, confidence, and courage can overcome stammering—and for that, TSS will always be there to help," says Poovarasan.

He thanks Mr. Manimaran, Agniraj, and all the TSS members for their role in his journey. He also actively encourages others who stammer to join TSS and emphasises the importance of regular speech practice.

B. Poovarasan – Chennai - Tamil Nadu

Email: poovarasankarthik@gmail.com

15

A SMILING STORY OF RK

CHILDHOOD

Rajkumar was born in December 1994 in Kanchipuram to a low-middle-class family. He was the second son. Both he and his elder brother had stammering issues from childhood. Their father also had a slight stammer.

Despite financial struggles, Rajkumar's parents ensured their children had good clothes, food, and education. Rajkumar considers having good-hearted parents his greatest wealth—far more valuable than being born into a wealthy family.

As a child, his friends didn't make much of his stammer, though some acquaintances mocked and teased him. Due to his inferiority complex, Rajkumar never participated in any competitions.

TEENAGE AND EARLY ADULTHOOD

Rajkumar grew up in a very limited social circle, which instilled in him a fear of rejection. Determined to prove himself, he took up dancing, becoming a devoted fan of Michael Jackson. He stepped far outside his comfort zone and performed MJ-style dances on stage. He even won a solo dance award from Gopinath on the

TV show *Neeya Naana*. Despite never attending dance school, he learned entirely by watching MJ's CDS.

He made sure no one saw him as a stammerer but rather as a dancer.

Like many 90s kids, he was shy around girls. He had a one-sided love, and instead of a love letter, he wrote a friendship letter. He would call the girl he liked on a ₹ 1-coin phone, listen to her voice, and cut the call without speaking, earning himself many emotional scars.

He was an average student throughout school and college. He studied in Tamil-medium government schools and later earned a Master of Commerce (M. Com).

After college, real life hit him. He feared job interviews and speaking in public, so he stuck to small, low-profile jobs—starting as a data entry operator and then trying for government jobs. Until the age of 24, he lived within his small social bubble.

ADULTHOOD

Due to his family's financial situation and wanting to overcome his fear of stammering, a friend introduced him to Mr. Murugan, an Accounts Manager, who helped him get a job as a junior accountant at Cavin Dairy Plant. He later worked at Yamaha, but local jobs weren't enough to sustain him financially.

Rajkumar decided to move to Chennai to change his life. There, he enrolled in SAP and Spoken English classes to develop his skills. After saving some money, he quit his small job and, at the age of 28, attended his first formal interview.

Due to stammering, he faced multiple rejections. However, after three months of relentless effort, in August 2023, he secured a job as a Finance Associate at a Chennai-based company. He's especially grateful to Thomas Kurippan (DGM Finance) and

Azhagappan (Head of Finance Operations), who welcomed him and gave him an opportunity, regardless of his stammer.

SPEECH PROGRESS THROUGH TSS

It was through the Tamil Super Speakers (TSS) group that Rajkumar realised stammering is not a disease—it's a habit and a mental pattern. He especially credits the Madurai stammering workshop, which brought him clarity and transformation. He is thankful to Agnee Raj for his role and also to Mr. Gnanasekar, who gave Rajkumar a chance to host a Chennai TSS meeting.

He joined other TSS members in daily online Google Meet sessions. On weekends, he and others would visit public places and talk to strangers to confront their fears. One of the proudest moments in his life came on October 22, International Stuttering Awareness Day (ISAD), when he got to speak as an RJ for a day on Chennai Radio Mirchi—a dream opportunity made possible by Mr. Manimaran. His mother's joy upon hearing that broadcast was beyond words.

TSS'S VISION AND RAJKUMAR'S GROWTH

The TSS group's goal is to help stammerers find the right path, support each other, and lead fulfilling lives. The group encourages continuous speech practice and participation in all group activities.

Rajkumar began discovering his inner strength only after moving to Chennai. The lesson he learned is that you cannot grow by staying in your comfort zone; ever since then, he has been trying new things constantly.

From someone who feared even hearing his name in school, he now confidently speaks in English at work. And yet, he considers this just the beginning—he looks ahead with confidence at a long and successful journey.

He expresses heartfelt thanks to his friends Subraja, Simbu, Ellappan, Pandian, Suresh, Jayavel, and Sai for always standing by him and never treating his stammer as a weakness.

RAJKUMAR'S ADVICE TO FELLOW STAMMERERS

Here, in his own words:

"To my dear stammering friends with beautiful voices, a few humble requests:

1. Remind yourself often—you are not alone.

2. Don't let anyone control you through your fear or anxiety.

3. Self-discipline is your ultimate saviour.

4. Learn to respect both experienced mentors and your inner voice.

5. Don't argue with those who disagree. Follow only what resonates with you.

6. Education is not just for earning money—it preserves your self-respect.

7. Be ever grateful to your parents and those who helped you.

8. Practice your speech daily—with the right companions.

9. Protect your childlike spirit.

10. Most importantly: *"There's no painting without a wall"—you need a strong body to pursue your dreams.*

Live and let live!

V. Rajkumar – Chennai - Tamil Nadu

Email: rajkvaradhan@gmail.com

16

BREAKING THE SILENCE

Near Sivakasi, in a village called A. Lakshmipuram, a baby boy was born to Mr. Balasubramanian and Mrs. Kartheswari on October 18, 1987. He was given two names: one by his grandmother as "Periyandavar" after the family deity, and another by his parents as "Vijayakumar" because he was their son. Little did they know then that the boy would struggle to pronounce his name due to stammering. His father also had a stammer, and Vijayakumar started stammering in his baby talk.

He completed his schooling with the name Vijayakumar. Though no one in school or college mocked him, his inferiority complex kept him from participating in sports or competitive exams.

Due to this inferiority, he feared he might be unable to express his feelings even when he liked a girl. Still, he managed to befriend the girl. As he didn't stammer while talking to friends, he eventually confessed his love to her. However, because of a delayed response and the girl's father's objection, the relationship didn't succeed.

After completing 12th grade, when someone asked about his exam score, Vijayakumar tried to respond but could only raise three fingers and stammer. The man jokingly asked if he had lost 3 marks out of 1000. Vijayakumar instantly replied (without stammering) that he had lost 300 marks. Everyone praised his quick wit and told him, "You've passed. Study well in college."

From 2004 to 2007, he studied BSc (Computer Science) at a college in Sattur, and from 2007 to 2010, he did his MCA at a college in Erode. During his first job interview, he couldn't even say his name and left midway due to mental stress. Later, with a recommendation, he joined a software company in Madurai.

In 2014, when looking for a bride, he insisted on talking to the girl directly and said, "I stammer. Did your family inform you? Do you want to marry me?"—he said all this without stammering. She agreed, and they got married.

Once, during a festival shopping trip to The Chennai Silks, he couldn't say his phone number when asked for it at billing. His wife stepped in and said the number. He was deeply disturbed by this incident.

Five years later, when he requested a job promotion, his manager said, "You don't speak well, so you'll only get a pay hike, not a promotion." Disheartened, he came across the Tamil Super Speakers (TSS) group in 2019 through Agnee Raj Anna (Big Brother).

After joining the group, he attended his first Self-Help Group (SHG) meeting at Rajaji Park, Madurai, where he gained the courage to accept his stammer. That same month, he attended a workshop for people who stammer and had the opportunity to speak in front of 50 people. This inspired him to talk openly about the group and its activities at home and work.

With that courage, he started speaking confidently in office meetings. Within a year of TSS training, his fear of stammering vanished. After six months of speech practice, he began speaking fluently. Friends and colleagues noticed his improvement. Now, he can say his name and phone number at shops without stammering, which gives him immense joy. His wife, too, acknowledged, "You're speaking very well now."

They said he lacked English fluency when he asked for a promotion again. He applied elsewhere and cleared the interview at a multinational company. Today, he is working there as an Assistant Manager.

Since he could not say his name in his first interview, he now speaks fluent English. People at work don't believe he ever had a stammer. Thanks to TSS, he now confidently speaks at every opportunity.

When Vijayakumar goes on trips with friends or family, he takes the lead in organising everything—from booking rooms to arranging vehicles to managing food. He even speaks up in situations where others hesitate. His confidence today is a result of persistence, self-belief, and the support of TSS.

Before marriage, his wife used to work, but now she is a homemaker. They have two sons. Today, Vijayakumar is happily settled in Madurai.

His advice to young people who stammer:

"First, talk about TSS with your family and friends. Share your training routines with them. If you're still in college or unmarried, use your free time to practice speaking. Grab every chance to speak—you'll improve quickly."

Vijayakumar expresses his heartfelt gratitude to Mr. Manimaran and Mr. Agnee Raj for raising awareness, guiding him with speech techniques, and supporting his journey. The TSS group, run by Mr. Manimaran and Mr. Agnee Raj, is a selfless initiative that helps individuals overcome stammering. The group operates on a free, service-based model.

B. Vijayakumar – Madurai - Tamil Nadu

Email: vijayan7777@gmail.com

17

HONEY POURED ON THE BITTER LIFE

Ravi Gnanaprakasam was born in 1973 in Nuwara Eliya, Sri Lanka. His father was a farmer and cook, while his mother helped her husband and cared for the home. Ravi was the tenth and youngest of ten siblings. Unfortunately, five of the ten siblings died within days of birth. Among the remaining five, Ravi had two elder brothers and two elder sisters. One brother died due to electrocution while working in the fields, and the other died in an accident. Today, only Ravi and his two elder sisters are alive.

When Ravi was eight years old, his father passed away suddenly on the previous day of the Pongal festival. Although Ravi's father was in good health, the cause of his death remains unclear to him.

Ravi studied from grades 1 to 5 in a local school in Nuwara Eliya. Then, from grades 6 to 11, he studied in a convent in Atton, about 40 km from his hometown. His purpose in joining the convent was to become a Christian Priest. During all these years, his mother worked in plantations and managed everything alone.

When he was a child, Ravi's mother applied herbal paste on his tongue and gave him water mixed with carom seeds in hopes of curing his stammering—but it didn't help. She passed away 18 years ago.

Like most people who stammer, Ravi went through embarrassing experiences in school. He couldn't say "present sir" properly during the roll call. However, he could sing and recite poems well. But once, during 10th grade, when he got on stage to recite a poem, he couldn't utter a single word. His classmates yelled at him, "Get down! Get down!" That incident deeply scarred him—he kept thinking about it for a whole month.

One of the teachers in that school, Mrs. Gnanaprakasam, once said, "You carry my name and yet you stammer—how embarrassing!" That, too, greatly affected him.

Another time, when he was hospitalised for fever, combined with cold and cough, he couldn't speak at all. When the doctor spoke to him on the first day, and he couldn't respond, the doctor assumed he was dumb and prescribed medication. The next day, when the doctor returned and heard Ravi speak, he exclaimed, "I thought you were dumb, but you're speaking!" Ravi replied, "I can speak, doctor—but I stammer." The doctor responded, "There's not much difference between stammering and being dumb" That comment from a doctor was deeply hurtful.

Due to the strict environment and discipline in the convent school in Atton, Ravi left after 11th grade and didn't pursue 12th grade. He later joined a clothing store in Colombo. Since he was more educated than others, he was appointed supervisor. However, he left the job after one and a half years due to the low salary.

Ravi had a passion for singing, and a girl who admired his singing fell in love with him. He married her on April 16, 1997. Since it was a love marriage, his wife already knew about his stammer. Exactly a year after their wedding, on April 16, 1998, they had their first daughter, followed by a son and another daughter.

Ravi joined a salon as an employee in 2000. He worked there until 2010, learning the trade. In 2011, he opened his salon, which he runs successfully.

Ravi joined the TSS (Tamil Super Speakers) group to overcome his stammering. He enthusiastically participated in every activity and continues to do so. He talks to every member of the group. The first call they receive is from Ravi whenever a new member joins. He practices speech exercises daily without fail and has completed **1,850 days** of consistent practice so far.

When asked about the reason behind his dedication, he said:

"Now I speak very well. I feel very happy. I speak confidently with everyone. I've become a new person. This transformation is because of the speech practice. That's why I'll continue it forever."

Seeing Ravi's dedication, Mr. Manimaran encouraged him to start the Sri Lanka Super Speakers group, which Ravi officially launched on July 28, 2021. Though the group has only nine members, its activities haven't picked up much, and the reason remains unclear.

NOTABLEACHIEVEMENT

In 2022, based on TSS's guidance, Ravi gave a 30-minute awareness speech on stammering in front of 60 students at a local Islamic school, proving his strength as a speaker.

A HEARTWARMING GESTURE

Two months ago, TSS leader Mr. Manimaran, his wife, and some friends visited Sri Lanka. When Ravi heard about it, he promised to meet them at the Colombo airport before they returned back to Chennai. Though the flight was at 5 p.m., and it would take

6–7 hours from his village to Colombo, Ravi took a night bus the day before and reached Colombo at dawn. He stayed at a lodge and met them at the airport by 2 p.m., bringing a large box of Sri Lanka's famous egg sweets to give Mr. Manimaran. They chatted for half an hour before Mr. Manimaran thanked him and departed.

ANOTHER KIND GESTURE

A few weeks later, when Yuvaraj, a former TSS member, came to Colombo, Ravi closed his shop for five days and personally welcomed him, showing him around Sri Lanka. This highlights Ravi's generosity and helpful nature.

IN HIS OWN WORDS

"I run a salon. Speaking is essential for this job. Despite stammering, I've managed it. After five years of speech practice, I'm happy to hear from others that I speak well. Stammering isn't just a habit—it's a tough battle. Every day, I fight within myself to speak like others. Now that it has come true, I enjoy my profession, time with family, and conversations with friends. I thank Mr. Manimaran and Mr. Agnee Raj from the bottom of my heart for training me."

HIS ADVICE TO PEOPLE WHO STAMMER

"Never feel guilty for stammering. Accept it openly—don't try to hide it for any reason. Practice speech every day without fail. If you do these things sincerely, anyone can speak well. "Life is meant to be lived!"

Ravi Gnanaprakasam – Sri Lanka

Email: sebastiongnanam@gmail.com

18

LET THEM LAUGH

I am Manimaran, currently living in Singapore with my family as a Permanent Resident. I am the next protagonist in this series of success stories.

I was born and raised in a small village called Narana Mangalam in the Tiruvarur district, Tamil Nadu. I was the fourth and youngest child in my family, born in 1975. I received my primary education at a local village school.

Growing up in a village with limited access to educational opportunities, financial difficulties, and a lack of electricity was already challenging. Additionally, I had to contend with the burden of stammering. It's pretty fascinating—even to me—how I overcame all those odds and reached my current position.

There is a particular joy in turning back the wheel of time and stirring up memories buried deep within me. I sincerely thank the authors for allowing me to rewind my memories in this book.

I am now nearing 50 years of age. My half-century-long journey of life has been deeply intertwined with the stammering issue. Life has been like slipping a foot for every step taken. At every turn, I've faced landmines named "stammering." I encountered a bottomless pit of despair whenever I tried to move forward, and this persistent speech problem. But instead of giving in with an "I can't," I pushed through and kept moving ahead.

Everyone's life journey has its share of hardships. If the road is rocky for others, it has been full of boulders for me. Compared to people who can speak fluently, those with stammering issues must work many times harder. Only those who can turn the mocking laughter and taunts into a hammer strong enough to break through the boulders can achieve success.

Did I have the strength to make that transformation? Not. On one side, I was running like a machine, pushed by the pressure to be a good son to my parents, a responsible husband to my wife, and a great father to my child. But on the other side, because of my stammering issue, I lived for many years like a mentally distressed person. I lacked consistency and determination in my actions. I was always timid, unable to make firm decisions in any situation. My life moved forward with constant anxiety, always worried about when I might get stuck again.

As an engineer, my job required frequent transfers. As I started to settle and introduce myself in a new place, it was time to move. The simplest question someone can ask is, "What is your name?" But if a person struggles to answer even that, what kind of life is that? When people across from me deliberately made fun of me, asking sarcastically, "What, did you forget your name?"—where could I vent the anger that built up inside me?

Generally, people with stammering issues tend to live within a self-imposed boundary, which becomes a kind of safety zone for them. As a result, many stammerers avoid progressing to the following stages of life. This is often mistaken for hesitation, but it is a deep-rooted fear. That very same fear travelled with me throughout my life.

As Kamal Haasan says in Thenali (A Tamil Movie),

"Fear of everything"

Fear of saying my name.

Fear of being called by name in class.

Fear of standing up to ask a question.

Fear of answering even when I knew the answer.

Fear when the phone rings.

Fear of wearing a watch, thinking someone might ask the time.

Fear of buying a bus ticket.

Fear of purchasing things at a shop.

Fear of speaking on stage. Fear of getting a promotion. Fear of asking for help.

Fear of relatives. Fear of attending family functions.

Fear of going to temples, thinking someone might ask my zodiac sign or birth star.

Fear of speaking. At times, even a fear of staying silent.

Fear of falling in love. And yes, even fear of getting married.

Fear... fear... fear...

Fear until the grave.

Was it the fear that caused the stammering, or was the stammering the cause of the fear?

It took me forty years to understand that.

My father was a government school teacher—a profession that involved speaking loudly and clearly to teach students. He was also a great speaker. My elder sister and two brothers were all good speakers as well. But why was I the only one with this stammering problem?

When I asked my mother about it after I became aware of my condition, she said, "You had seizures when you were a child, and I gave you a lot of *vasambu* (sweet flag, a traditional herb). That's when your stammering started." Later, I realised she said that out of ignorance.

Only over time did I understand that stammering can develop from observing and being influenced by another person who stammers. That's when I suspected that it might have started with a relative—an older brother-like figure—who often visited our home and had a stammer himself.

In general, village environments are often characterised by mockery and teasing. Friends, relatives, and just about everyone ridiculed me quite a bit in my childhood. They would laugh when I started speaking—even when I wasn't stammering. As a result, I began stammering on words I could otherwise say fluently.

School life is challenging for all students who stammer. I was no exception. Perhaps the teachers might have ignored me if I had been an average student. But I was a top-performing student—until I lost that spot. I struggled a lot during school.

After every lesson, I was expected to stand up and read aloud. Fearing that I would stammer and my classmates would laugh, I constantly reminded the teacher, "Sir, I have a stammer." But if they still made me read, and I stammered and others laughed, I'd end up brooding the whole day, staring blankly at the blackboard. At that age, I wasn't mature enough to understand or cope with my situation.

Sometimes, I even wish I were mute. Life would be so much more peaceful, I thought. As poet Kannadasan once wrote, *"Being mute brings a certain peace; being poor, too, brings a kind of peace."* He so deeply understood and articulated the sorrow that comes from one's helplessness—that's why he is known as the "King of Poets."

From 6th to 10th grade, I studied at the government school where my father worked as a teacher. Being a "teacher's son" in a village school came with special privileges—extra attention, praise, and the spotlight—all of which can inflate your pride. But they also create high expectations and tremendous pressure. My stammering significantly worsened during this phase. Since the teachers were familiar with me, I felt more at ease speaking openly.

In that school, during roll call, the teachers didn't call out each student's name. Instead, students had to say their names and add "Present, sir." The teachers had enough work already! If you spoke out of order or missed your turn, they would scold you harshly. Imagine my situation—just saying "Present, sir" felt like it took ages. And on top of that, I had to say, "Manimaran Present, sir" without missing the timing!

The moment the class teacher opened the attendance register; all the students would rapidly start announcing their names in sequence like a speeding train. If I failed to speak at the right time, everything would come to a screeching halt. The teacher would glare at me with red eyes and snap, "Who's that boy?" And there I'd be, frozen in my salute, stammering and struggling. As usual, the class would burst into laughter. No punishment, though—I was the teacher's son! From the next day onward, the boy sitting next to me would also say my attendance along with his.

I used to stammer a lot when reciting poems, such as the Thirukkural or English poems, from memory in class. So, the teachers told me it was enough if I just wrote and submitted them. At the time, those exemptions felt like privileges. However, I later realized that they were not just foolish accommodations—they actually exacerbated my stammering problem.

I joined a different school for 11th grade. The environment was completely different—everything was new. No special privileges.

I had to stand up and read aloud, like everyone else, and recite the *Thirukkural* from memory in front of the class. Despite the struggle, I had to study hard to fulfil my parents' newly kindled ambition of seeing me become a doctor or an engineer. The pressure was immense, and so was the stammering.

While I was in 12th grade, an unforgettable incident occurred. A speech competition was announced, and each class had to send participants. Since our "First Group" students were all busy preparing intensely for the board exams, no one volunteered. Annoyed, our Tamil teacher picked up the attendance register, read out four names at random, and said, "These four will participate," and left. My bad luck—my name was among the four.

Some of my concerned friends immediately suggested that I explain my situation to the teacher. I hesitantly approached him and tried to explain, but he said, "Your name has already been submitted." If this had been my father's school, I could have written and submitted my speech. However, there was no such option now. There's no way to swap me out, either. So, I resigned myself to the reality—I would have to step on that stage.

There were two days left. I couldn't sleep well, couldn't eat properly, and I hadn't prepared anything. And even if I did, would I be able to deliver it fluently? I had zero faith in that. My secret plan was simple: I would start with, "Literature is indeed a pleasure," give an example, recite a *Kural*, and quickly exit the stage. That was my big escape strategy.

The day came. My name was called. I climbed onto the stage. I clasped my hands behind me and stared at the back wall to avoid looking at the audience. I felt a bit courageous. I successfully said the first sentence. Then I started with "For example" and tried to recite the *Kural*. It didn't come. A whole minute passed. The laughter began to bubble up from the audience. I was mortified. I didn't have the courage even to glance down. I quickly said, "Thank you," and rushed off the stage.

For a whole week after that, I felt too ashamed to look anyone in the eye in class.

But during that period, I had an intense inner fire. Each time I stammered and felt humiliated; I channelled all my focus into academics. I believed that studying hard was the best weapon to retaliate against the society that mocked me. In 10th grade, I was the "School First." I believed education was my armour, shielding me from all those taunts and jabs. That very belief, I have no doubt, is what ultimately led me to Singapore.

Back then, getting admission into an engineering college was like chasing a unicorn. At the school I attended, only one student would typically earn that opportunity each year. During morning assembly, the principal would announce the name of that lucky student, offer congratulations, and advise everyone else to follow in their footsteps. All the students would applaud. The chosen student's name would be displayed proudly at the school entrance with the message, *"You have brought pride to our school."* It was an actual **goosebumps moment**. Who wouldn't dream of that?

Even in 1993, when I was studying, only one student was given that prestigious opportunity. During the morning assembly, that name was read out amidst loud applause:

"From our school's 12th-grade Mathematics stream, the student Manimaran has secured admission to Tiruchirappalli Regional Engineering College..."

Yes—that was me.

I wasn't there during that goosebumps moment, as I had already joined the college. But through that success, I felt I had transformed from "Stammering Manimaran" to "Engineer Manimaran"—silencing all those who once mocked me. That moment, when I turned shame and pain into fuel for success, remains unforgettable in my life.

Everyone has dark chapters in their life. It's part of our life journey. For me, that chapter was my college life.

Until then, the idea was that if you studied and wrote well, you would get good marks. But in college, I had reached the next level—where *you had to speak.* That shook my self-confidence. Especially as someone who had studied in Tamil medium, transitioning to a fully English-based curriculum was highly challenging. My interest in academics began to fade.

I naturally disliked English. For someone who stammered even while speaking Tamil, English felt like a curse. It topped my list of "things I hate." I firmly believe that *one language alone is enough.*

There were many North Indian students in college. You had to communicate with them *only in English.* That wasn't possible for me. Watching my fellow Tamil classmates speak fluently in English with them gave me an intense sense of inferiority. As I said earlier, I couldn't break out of that mental cage.

College days were also a time of youthful emotions. There were several girls in my class. At that age, it's normal for glances to be exchanged occasionally. For young men, it's a matter of pride to appear cool and stylish in front of girls. But the fear that my stammer would ruin that image made me highly anxious.

The first semester began. Professors started taking classes, and as they entered, they'd say, "Introduce yourself." One by one, students stood up and confidently shared their names and hometowns.

A new kind of fear and nervousness gripped me. The hall was large, and the distance between the professor and the students was considerable. My turn came. I stood up and started, "I am..."—and then couldn't say my name. My throat closed up. Nervousness spread across my face. My eyes twitched. My jaw clenched. No sound came out despite repeated attempts.

Everyone turned to look at me. The impatient professor asked in English, "Why? Did you forget your name?" I couldn't understand him. I wasn't in a state to understand anything. And those classmates who *did* understand burst out laughing, shouting "Kol!" (an expression of mockery). The classroom returned to normal. But for me... it was the height of humiliation.

Gone was my fiery determination to turn shame into fertiliser for growth. I somehow stuttered out my name and took a seat. My ears rang. I was overcome by sorrow I couldn't name. I bowed my head and began to cry silently.

In the following classes, the same humiliation repeated. The same ridicule, the same laughter. To them, I had become a joker. That's what I believed. I didn't have the mental strength to either overcome the shame or convince myself it wasn't shameful at all. That's the weakness shared by many who stammer.

I was on the edge of despair. I couldn't find the old, confident Manimaran anymore. I knew it myself. What remained was a spineless, timid introvert with shaking knees.

If this was my present, what about my future? I had to complete engineering in four years. I had to be ready for campus interviews. The biggest hurdle: Group Discussions—face-to-face with my worst fear. I had to speak fluently in those. In *English*, no less!

How was any of that even possible?

That very thought shattered what little self-confidence I had left.

The result? I began to isolate myself slowly. I only interacted with a select few classmates. A growing inferiority complex crept in—was I even fit to study engineering? While others chatted freely with the girls in class, I shrank away from everyone, ashamed of my limitations.

A wounded heart... what else could it do? I picked up the habit of smoking. I started going to the cinema frequently with friends. Thankfully, my body didn't tolerate alcohol, so I never developed a drinking habit. The anger I had towards society and the frustration I had towards myself—driven by that, I knowingly made many mistakes. I became someone I began to hate.

I started skipping classes frequently—especially during the first week of every semester. The reason? Just one: *"Introduce yourself."*

I had a bad reputation among the professors. My interest in studies started to decline. The result? Backlogs—many of them. Even before I could clear one semester's arrears, a new row of backlogs would begin in the following semester. I reached a point of utter despair where even thoughts of suicide crossed my mind. And all of it was because of this miserable stammering problem— it had turned me into someone mentally unstable.

By then, I had only one goal: to somehow get through the four years. It was one of the top engineering colleges at the time— and still is. In the final semester, 100% job placement was the norm through campus interviews. But for me, interviews were a nightmare. Though I initially avoided them, as time passed and every other student in my department got placed, I had no choice but to participate in a few interviews.

When the interviewer asked questions, even though I knew the answers, the fear would paralyse my words. One interviewer, visibly irritated, said, "Why did you even study engineering? You've wasted a seat." That wasn't the first time I had heard such a thing.

In one of the practical sessions, during a viva exam, even though I knew the answer, I couldn't express it. One professor, unaware of my condition, fanned his record book in frustration and scolded me with the same harsh comment. That day, I made a decision. No matter how hard I prepared, my stammer would always get me scolded. So why bother preparing at all? You're going to get shouted at anyway—so go ahead and shout. That was my new mindset.

College ended. While every other student walked out with a job offer in hand, I walked out with a handful of backlogs. I didn't know what to do next. I didn't want to stay at home either. I had to complete my engineering degree. All my friends had left for jobs in Bangalore, Hyderabad, and other parts of North India. I had missed the golden opportunity of campus interviews. The future looked dark. I stood unarmed on the battlefield of life.

Then, I made a firm decision. I had gained more wounds than wisdom in college. Let me shut the chapter on those dark college days. Let me awaken the self-confidence and motivation I had in school and begin the next phase of life from there. With that resolve, I took some money from home, bought groceries, and left for Chennai with a couple of bags in late 1997 after finishing college.

My sanctuary of light was a 10'x10' room in Pazhavanthangal, Chennai, where my second elder brother was staying. I cooked, washed, and slept there. Monthly rent: ₹350. Only one toilet—for 30 people. Every morning, there'd be a long queue.

Every day, I carried my bio-data and went from company to company in search of a job. At that time, finding a job in Chennai was highly challenging. Very few industries. The IT sector isn't yet established. Small factories only hired ITI or diploma holders.

Engineering graduates were outright rejected. You couldn't even get past the security gate at big companies. Four months passed like that. I didn't want to go back to my hometown.

Nor did I want to take up any random job just for the money—I could have opened a small shop back home if that were the case.

On one side, backlogs burdened me on the other, unemployment. But I didn't give up. I made a decision: *whether I live or die, it will be in Chennai.*

After four months, I got a call from my elder brother in Pondicherry. He had already spoken to the manager of his company's Chennai branch on my behalf and instructed me to join immediately. My brother had a good reputation there. I couldn't contain my excitement—my first job, my first salary. My mind flew with imagination. I even made a list of things I wanted to buy. When I looked at myself in the mirror while combing my hair, my face looked bright. Maybe it was the light—or perhaps it was hope.

My brother told me not to discuss the salary with the manager—he'd take care of it.

Salary? I thought, "Even if I'm just given tea twice a day and bus fare, that's enough—I'll work the whole month without pay." With that mindset, I set out the following day to the address my brother had given.

The manager took all the certificates I had and started interviewing me. I hadn't expected that at all. My brother had sent me there to *join*, not to face another test! Why this sudden trial? It felt like fate was deliberately targeting my weakness. Still, I hesitantly introduced myself.

The first thing he asked—in English—was, "Do you stammer?" My throat immediately closed up. He had hit right on the nerve. As he continued questioning, I stammered and struggled to find a response. The manager lost his temper. He threw my certificates down and shouted, "You studied at REC, and you don't even know this?"

That was nothing new to me.

What next? I figured he'd say the usual line: "You wasted an engineering seat."

So I sat there quietly.

But then he threw something else at me—something more painful than any insult.

"I'm not giving you this job for your sake. I'm giving it because your brother's blood runs in your veins."

That line deeply wounded me. Yes, I stammer. Yes, I can't speak fluently.

But if he didn't think I was fit for the job, he could've just rejected me. That's the norm.

But who gave him the right to insult me like that? What authority did he have?

For the first time, I felt genuine anger. Still, since it was my brother's company, I left without saying anything.

That evening, after the manager spoke to my brother, I got a scolding over the phone. But my brother still said, "He's going to hire you anyway; go and join." I refused. I didn't give a reason. That moment had struck at my self-respect.

Back to job-hunting again. With a friend's help, I got a job at a welding workshop in Padi-Vanniyar Street. A salary was barely equal to a helper's—₹1000. But for me, it felt like a thousand gold coins gifted by the gods.

After rent and food, I had ₹200 left in hand.

Archimedes once said, *"Give me a place to stand, and I will move the Earth."* That workshop was my place. Salary didn't matter. My only goal was to learn. With the small experience I gained there, I moved to a CNC (Computer Numerical Control) company.

I soon learned that having CNC experience made it easier to secure jobs abroad.

And I began to realise—that was the path meant for me.

Four years passed. I had switched to eight companies. Finally, I cleared all my backlogs and got my engineering degree certificate. All the closed doors began to open.

I had a peculiar habit—whatever I learned, I immediately wanted to teach others.

Not just because my father was a teacher but because I genuinely loved teaching.

There were two benefits to this:

1. It helped me deeply internalise what I learned.

2. It slowly helped reduce my stammering.

I taught many friends CNC for free—and, in the process, made many new friends.

Many of my colleagues had started going abroad—especially to Singapore.

One by one, they left. That desire began to take root in me, too.

There was another reason. In all the companies I worked for, I was able to excel only in physically demanding roles. When I got jobs like supervisor or engineer, I couldn't perform well—because those roles required strong communication skills.

And my stammering stood as a massive barrier. As a result, I couldn't command higher salaries. But my friends abroad told me, "Out there, it's not about talk—it's about skill."

That gave me hope. And I decided that *Singapore is where I belong.*

There's also a side story in my long list of rejections. While I was in school, one of my father's colleagues—and later, a relative by marriage—had planned to arrange my marriage to his daughter. Both families had planted that idea in our young minds.

As soon as I got an engineering seat, the girl's family confirmed it. Later, she got into teacher training and joined a government school. A government job, after all! So, my family decided she was the one.

But here came the twist—while she was earning in the tens of thousands, I was only earning in the thousands. So, her family told mine, "If your son likes, let him marry our other daughter—she's at home now. We'll marry the teacher's daughter to someone better." The teacher didn't object to this.

I thought—*Do thousands always remain thousands? Won't they become lakhs someday?*

This body, built on rejection and pain—what will this fresh rejection do to me? But I didn't break down. I didn't beg.

My ambition at the time was different. I wanted to stand tall in front of them and say, *"You once said no to me. Now I say—I don't want your daughter."* That fire kept me going.

"That's all fine... but if I wanted to go abroad, I had to face an interview. And that too, with a foreign client. How was I going to handle that with my stammering issue?"

My bio-data had been passed to several agents through friends. One day, I received a call from an agent in K.K. Nagar, saying that a client from Singapore would be arriving the next day and asking me to come in the morning. I went with determination—not to repeat the mistakes I had made during my college campus interview.

It was for an engineering position. Around 50 candidates had come. As the saying goes, *"Dragging a mountain with a thread"*—it felt like that. I joined the process with the attitude: *Let's see where this goes.*

Out of the 50, only five, including me, were shortlisted for the written test. Next was the face-to-face interview. I decided to use a strategy. The person interviewed was Chinese. On one side, my English was broken; on the other, his accent was hard to follow. But I figured I could catch a few technical words in his questions and build my answers around that. I resolved to speak confidently, even if I stammered, and mixed Tamil and English.

Questions were asked. I caught some CNC-related keywords. That was enough. I began speaking loudly and confidently, regardless of my stammering. I never hesitated. I didn't say, *"I don't know."* I could sense that the interviewer liked my approach.

The interview ended.

Whether I got selected or not didn't matter—this was the first interview where I didn't get scolded. That made me happy. I couldn't help but wonder why I hadn't done this back in college.

Ultimately, I was the only candidate selected. The company's boss handed me the appointment order right there. Within ten days, my visa arrived. The salary? Eight times more than that teacher's. I had to pay the agent a hefty fee. I informed my relatives. I especially made sure to whisper the news into the postman's ear—like a poetic twist of fate.

But things don't usually go that smoothly for me, do they?

Wherever I step, fate lays landmines.

Yes, that was the time of the 9/11 attacks in the US.

The Singapore company said its position was unstable.

Ticketing got delayed. I waited... and waited.

Not one or two—but ten whole months passed.

I had already resigned from my job.

I couldn't take another job, because they might call at any time.

Later, I realised they were never going to call.

I'd been rejected.

Shouldn't I at least get my money back?

It wasn't until ten months later that I realised the agent had been playing a game with me.

I couldn't return home. Too many questions would be asked.

Just when I was confused about what to do next, luck knocked at my door. Literally.

Someone knocked on the door of the room where I was staying. "Is Manimaran here?" he asked. He explained he was from another agency. When he went to Singapore, he'd heard from a friend that they needed a CNC programmer. That friend gave him my *old address*.

When he couldn't find me there, he tracked down my new address—and came to see me.

TEN DAYS LATER, I WAS IN SINGAPORE!

Take a look at how it all turned out...

The job, the salary, the work environment—everything was exactly what I had dreamed of. No one made a big deal about my stammering. By the sixth month, I had purchased land and held a housewarming ceremony in my hometown. During my brother's wedding, the respect I received from relatives was beyond anything I had ever imagined.

Money speaks.

Interestingly, the *teacher's family attempted* to rekindle the relationship. But my family had already given them a fitting reply.

In Singapore, I continued my passion for teaching. I began offering free classes at home to friends in my field. More than 20 would attend—some were keen, some yawned, some dozed off. I didn't care.

I needed to speak loudly.

I wanted to reduce my fear of stammering.

To me, those 20 people were like "practice props."

In my four years in Singapore, I never once felt worried about my stammering.

Even when I stammered severely, no one seemed to care.

That made me forget I even had such an issue.

But then... the next test came—in the form of marriage.

My family started looking for a bride. We thought, with a good salary, own house, and strong educational background, finding a bride would be easy.

Surely, stammering wouldn't be a big deal anymore.

But I had forgotten something—*the girl's choice.*

I stayed quiet during the initial meetings, thinking that the elders would talk and settle things. My silence had a reason—I didn't want to embarrass myself by stammering in front of everyone.

I figured I'd talk to the girl privately afterwards. As soon as I saw her, I liked her.

I could tell she expected me to say something. But I didn't. Once I got her number, the first thing I did after returning home was call her.

I shared some details about myself. Her first question: "Do you stammer?" I didn't dare to admit it outright. I deflected. She cut the call—and the proposal—right there.

This happened three times.

In each case, I knew clearly—the rejections were because of my stammering.

What could I do? No matter how high you climb in life, stammering follows like a shadow.

It hangs over your head like a sword, ready to fall at any time. Fed up, I told my family: "You decide on the girl. I'm going back to Singapore."

Then, finally, a marriage proposal was fixed. Only my photo was shared initially. One of the girl's relatives was living in Singapore, and at their request, I went and met him in person. The girl had completed her engineering degree and was working as a lecturer at Shanmugha College of Technology in Thanjavur.

All the usual formalities and rituals followed, and even the engagement date was decided. Her parents insisted that I come and see her before things progressed. It was her life, after all. What if I didn't like her later?

Despite financial constraints, and because I was about to marry this person, I agreed and travelled to meet her.

By then, I had let go of many expectations about how a wife should be. All I wanted was for the marriage to happen.

As usual, I stayed quiet. The girl's family liked that about me. She, too, was silent. I made sure to get her phone number before returning to Singapore. With the sense of confidence that she was my future wife, I boldly called her. I had barely spoken for two minutes when the question came: "Do you stammer?"

Perhaps I should have told her beforehand. That would've been the honest thing to do.

Or even then, I could have just said "Yes." But instead, I dodged it, saying: *"Only occasionally..."* I don't know what she thought, but she started avoiding me. Eventually, she stopped answering my calls. And finally, the message came from her family: "The girl is not interested."

I was shattered. My life, which had been moving smoothly like thread unwinding from a spool, was suddenly shaken by the earthquake of marriage rejections. I started isolating myself again—I even avoided talking to my parents. Eventually, they reached out and inquired about what had happened. I broke down crying and said: "Why is this happening only to me?"

I declared firmly: "I will never get married. No one should ever bring up this topic again."

They wouldn't have expected that. They had arranged marriages for many others—why couldn't they find the right girl for their son? They were heartbroken. After several months of persuasion, I finally agreed to consider marriage again—but with conditions.

I said:

"I won't meet or speak with the girl or her family. I will come only to tie the *thali* (wedding thread). Find someone who agrees to this, and go meet them." The woman who agreed to this is now my wife and life partner. Before and after the wedding, she never once asked about my stammering.

Four years later, our son was born. I had crossed many phases of life. I felt like, from this point on, I could manage whatever came. But then came another thunderbolt. My son, who spoke fluently until the age of four, began to stammer. I was shaken.

I thought, *"Let my stammer end with me—but why this new punishment?"* Would my son have to endure the same struggles that I did? I couldn't believe it. Was this a hereditary curse? "Why only me?" This question gnawed at me constantly.

In the village where I was born, there was a family with seven brothers who all stammered. But none of their children inherited it. So, I had always believed it wouldn't be passed on.

My family assured me: *"He'll grow out of it."* But I didn't have that confidence. Just like I feared, my son's stammer only grew worse. Then, I made a firm decision. My parents never made any real effort to help me with my stammer. They weren't even concerned about it.

Later, when I tried to help myself, we didn't have the financial means. But I was not going to let that happen to my son. I resolved that, no matter the cost, I would address this issue at its root.

I began searching for treatment options in Singapore. Eventually, I found a well-known speech therapist—one who spoke Tamil fluently. I immediately took my son to see him. He said, *"There's no issue. We can fix it in two months. Just sign up for two packages."* Each package was 10 sessions. The cost: ₹2 lakhs per package. I paid a total of ₹4 lakhs. We completed 20 sessions. However, instead of improving, my son's stammering got **worse**. When I asked the doctor about it, he gave a vague explanation. That's when I realised that even *though I had a basic understanding of stammering, this therapist didn't have a clue.*

After that, I became even more committed to learning about stammering. I began to understand it better. I realised something crucial: If my son had grown up surrounded by extended family and spoken with them regularly, he would have picked up language naturally. But he grew up watching me only. And who would he imitate if not me?

That's when I understood—the fault was mine. I should have fixed my stammer before he was born. I hadn't. But now, at least, I had to make an effort. I wanted him to see me speak fluently and confidently—every single day. Only then would his fear go away and faith grow in its place. With that clarity, I started searching online.

That's when I came across an announcement about a free training group for people who stammer on WhatsApp. Generally, there is no direct or guaranteed cure for stammering.

Many people exploit this by offering fake treatments for money. I had already had bitter experiences like that. So, when I saw a group offering free training, I knew it had to be a genuine act of service. And if it came from a place of genuine understanding—then that was where the real learning would happen.

I immediately called the number mentioned in the announcement. The name of that group was the Tamil Super Speaker Group (TSS). Its Managing Director, Agnee Raj, asked me about my problem and then patiently explained, over a phone call lasting nearly an hour and a half, what stammering is, why it happens, how it can be managed, and what techniques can help. All the questions that had confused me for so many years finally got answered that day.

For the first time, a ray of hope lit up my face.

I also learned about Mr. V. Manimaran (Chennai), who founded the group and has been tirelessly working towards building a stammer-free society. I was amazed. In a world full of consultants who ask about your problem for 30 minutes and then charge thousands in fees, their selfless service stunned me.

By sheer coincidence, not only do we share the same name—Manimaran—but he also studied at the Tiruchirapalli Regional Engineering College, the very same college where I studied. That added another layer of amazement.

I immediately joined the group and began practicing the techniques they suggested. Generally, a person who stammers avoids befriending another stammerer. They treat them almost like a rival. I was no exception. But after joining TSS, I spoke openly to another person who stammered—for the first time. I began to form friendships with other members and started talking to them daily over the phone. We shared our challenges, our experiences, and the struggles we had each faced.

This group became a pressure valve, a relief system—a place where I could finally offload all the burdens I'd carried for years. I owe a lifelong debt of gratitude to the Tamil Super Speaker group. Let me explain why.

When we have a high fever, we visit a doctor. He might give us the same tablet he gives everyone. The fever goes away, and we think of him as a god at that moment.

For the doctor, it's just his job. He gets paid. But here, in this group, the trainers not only teach us the techniques—they check in to ensure we're doing them correctly. For them, it's not a job, it's not about income, and they don't receive awards either. Yet they do it with total dedication, expecting nothing in return.

If they teach ten people and even one of them says, "I can speak well now,"—that joy is their reward. Even when someone says, "I trained with that therapist and paid money, but it didn't help," they still warmly say, *"No problem, join our group."* Why? Because they don't want others to suffer the way they did.

Having spoken with many speech therapists—including those educated abroad—I can confidently say this:

They do not truly understand stammering. They may excel at treating children who don't speak at all or those with general speech delays. But stammering is a different beast. There is no proven medical treatment for it. Only someone who has personally struggled with stammering—and overcome it through the proper methods—can guide others effectively. That's why I say with conviction: The training offered by this group is the best. The understanding you gain here is equivalent to a professional degree in speech pathology.

Just before the COVID-19 pandemic, I joined this group. I was 44 years old. That's nearly 40 years of pain. Now I had found relief—would I ever let it go?

They told me: *"Practice breathing and speaking exercises every morning for at least 30 minutes."* I practiced for two hours.

I used to wake up at 7 am, shower, and go to work. Now, I started waking up at 5 am. I split my time into:

* Breathing exercises

* Speech drills

* Reading news aloud

* Reciting poems slowly

* And finally, speaking with fellow TSS friends over the phone

If I had time during the day, we would make conference calls, practice techniques, and discuss recent speech challenges. And then fate helped me again—I got two months of COVID leave. I thought, ' How can I best use this time *for my speech training?* '

But more than just the exercises, something else elevated my progress—the daily topic challenge introduced by Agnee Raj. Each day, he would post a topic and ask us to speak on it for at least three minutes, then post the audio in the WhatsApp group. Despite his heavy workload, he would listen to each recording and give encouraging feedback or suggestions.

The first time I tried, I barely managed 3 minutes and 30 seconds. I stammered a lot. My speech and thoughts weren't aligned. When I thought silently, ideas flowed. But when I started speaking, all I could think about was not stammering, so I forgot what I wanted to say. Even the words I had found during my silent planning didn't come to mind when I spoke.

It was a strange and frustrating issue, but I realised it only while doing those topics. I made a new resolution: Living abroad, I didn't have a platform to speak in Tamil, so this would be my stage. Before speaking on any topic, I would write notes. Then, I would begin.

First, I spoke for 3 minutes... then 5... then 10... and 30 minutes. Eventually, I stopped using notes altogether. What is the longest I've spoken on a topic? 58 minutes. And I stopped only because *I decided that was enough!*

The amazing part?

No matter how long I spoke, Agnee Raj always made time to listen and provide feedback.

Previously, I couldn't even speak long sentences. Due to stammering, my longest sentence would be just five words. I pushed myself to attempt complex, extended thoughts during these speeches.

I never posted my first recording right away. I listened to it and analysed it. If I wasn't happy, I deleted it and recorded it again. Sometimes, I spend three hours preparing a 15-minute talk.

And the result?

Today, I can speak for over an hour on any topic without notes. My speech matches the speed of my thoughts.

There was a time when, while speaking to friends or relatives over the phone, they'd say, Say *something... anything."* They interrupt and say, *"Let me speak for a minute!"*

I don't pause between sentences. I speak faster than many fluent speakers.

This change—speaking fluently despite having a stammer—is my most significant victory.

And it was made possible by the Tamil Super Speaker (TSS) group.

Now, even my wife hesitates to argue with me—what more significant win could there be?

I practice my techniques openly. Only the reading practice, which is quite loud, is in a separate room. It's so loud that neighbours come over to check what's going on.

My son has been observing my practice closely. Initially, I felt sad that my stutter might have influenced him. Now, I see it differently. I believe my son *absorbed* my stammering and, in doing so, motivated me to take this training seriously. He is the driving force behind my journey. And now, I feel confident that I can help him by giving him the understanding he needs to overcome this.

Our mind is the biggest procrastinator. It permanently blocks attempts to improve. It whispers, *"Let's try tomorrow..."* Every time you try to act, the mind says, *"The doctor's not in—don't knock on the door."* Please don't listen to it.

Knock harder. If necessary, break down the door.

Because this training isn't something you do for a day or two, it must be done consistently for weeks and months. A boulder doesn't crack with a single hammer strike. You need to keep hitting. Even if it breaks on the tenth blow, the first nine weren't in vain—each one sent a shockwave through the rock. That's how training works.

Many people quit after a week or two, expecting instant results. However, stammering isn't a one-week habit—it has been deeply embedded in their subconscious for many years.

How can it go away in just one week? Some people don't hit hard enough or consistently.

But they expect the boulder to break on the second blow. How is that possible?

Even now, I stammer sometimes—I can feel it when I speak. Others might not notice, but I know. Sometimes, they do notice.

But I'm not worried. Before, I used to feel ashamed. Now, I'm mature enough to *invite* that shame—it pushes me to work harder.

Earlier, during arguments with friends, they'd say, "*You're stammering too much these days...*" That was a psychological attack, and it used to shake me.

Even if someone says that when I speak fluently, I respond, "So what?" Let's continue." That clarity came from this group.

Now, I have no trouble speaking in Tamil, my mother tongue. In English, I still stammer in some places—but I believe that's more due to a lack of vocabulary than a problem with my speech. Wherever I lack confidence, I notice stammering. So, I'm now following the same rigorous training in English that I did for Tamil. Soon, I'll conquer that, too.

Every time I feel humiliated, I think of these lines:

"Oh, human! Tear your heart and plant a seed – it will grow into a tree.

Shame and failure – they are all manure.

Only stones that endure the chisel become statues.

Only hearts that bear pain attain lasting peace."

Are there not people who have achieved great things despite having permanent disabilities? In comparison, ours is a temporary challenge. We will overcome it.

In my view, those who stammer must strive for more than fluency among fluent speakers.

Because that is not only *our* victory but also a hammer blow to society's negative views about people who stammer.

Until recently, I was a machine operator/programmer. Now, I've advanced to the role of Engineer. The burden has been lifted. The path is clear.

What is there to fear now? I've confidently begun the next chapter of my journey toward my goals.

Here are a few suggestions from me for those doing stammering practice:

1. Do your speech practice early in the morning.

2. The mind and body are calm after a good sleep. Don't postpone it until after a bath or breakfast—you may skip it altogether.

3. Practice loudly—especially while reading.

4. Speaking requires coordination between the jaw, tongue, nose, vocal cords, and the respiratory system. Loud practice activates and strengthens all these areas.

5. When you feel lazy, try for two minutes.

6. That's enough to get momentum. Shame and pain will flash before your eyes, and you'll start practicing with passion.

7. Consistency is everything.

8. Missing one or two days is fine. However, many drop out completely after a short break, thinking, "I haven't improved much, so *why bother?*" Don't think like that.

9. Like a bodybuilder who trains regularly to stay fit, make this a lifelong habit.

10. It can turn you from a stammerer into a confident public speaker.

11. The group's core practices are essential.

12. Additionally, try other speaking methods, such as reading aloud or talking on the phone with members. One method doesn't work for everyone. Find what works best for you.

13. Body language is crucial.

14. Wave your hands and move your head while speaking—it can help reduce stammering. Place the phone in front of you instead of holding it and talk as if you're having a real conversation. This will build fluency in real-life situations.

15. Listen to your recordings.

16. After speaking on a topic, play it back. If you're not happy, delete it and try again. Often, you think you stammered—but it sounds smooth. That motivates you. Praise yourself—*"Well done!"* That small joy lays the foundation for greater confidence.

17. If you stammer unexpectedly in public, observe your reaction.

18. How long does the effect last? If it bothers you the next day, you're still in the early stages. If you're able to forget it immediately, you're making progress.

19. Life is very short. Don't waste your time constantly thinking about your stammering.

R. Manimaran – Singapore

email: rmmsg2000@gmail.com

19

OPPORTUNITIES POURING INTO HIS HOUSE

Alphonse was born on June 5, 1987, in Kalaiyar Koil, Sivagangai district, to Mr. Santhanam and Mrs.Savariammal. He has an elder sister. His father was also a stammerer, and by age five, Alphonse began mimicking his father's speech, which eventually led to him stammering as well.

He studied in an English-medium school until the 5th grade, but due to financial difficulties, he shifted to a Tamil-medium Christian school for grades 6–8. He fondly recalls this as his favourite school.

He was a well-respected student among his teachers. Once, in 7th grade, a Tamil teacher scolded him for a minor mistake and said, "Even God has measured everything carefully—that's why He made you a stammerer." That statement scarred him deeply. However, the same teacher later started liking him, seemingly realising her mistake. Alphonse graduated from that school as the top student.

From grades 9 to 12, he studied at Don Bosco and still considers it his least favourite school. In 10th grade, when the school picked a few students for special training, no one noticed him. Still, he studied, determined to be state first, and to everyone's surprise, he became school first, earning pride from his parents. This remains a moment of pride in his life.

Since childhood, Alphonse loved exploring things like a scientist. His father often said he would become one someday. At one point, Alphonse dreamed of studying MCA and going to the U.S. During his school days, he discovered a spark of creativity and declared he wanted to become a film director. That ambition reduced his interest in academic studies. Due to his stammer, he became an introvert and a target of jokes among classmates.

While attending a campus interview in Madurai during his final year of Diploma (ECE), he was among the top 20 out of 1500 to clear the written test. But during the final interview, he stammered severely. The panel told him, "You must speak fluently for this job. Please look for something else." Despite coming so far, he was heartbroken. He felt that his life could've been different if he had gotten that job—with foreign travel and good earnings. In 2008, Alphonse moved to Chennai to find a job.

He tried various ways to control his stammer. He tried Siddha medicine and vilvam leaf powder. In 10th grade, his father sent him to a psychologist in Coimbatore for a week. There, he was taught reading practice and relaxation techniques. He was told to stretch the first word slowly while speaking. This made him sound like a Sri Lankan Tamil or a Malayali. When applying for a passport, even the verification officer asked if he was Sri Lankan. Alphonse had to explain it was just part of his speech therapy—a funny memory today.

What he liked most about TSS (Tamil Super Speakers) was that it required no modulation changes—to speak slowly and steadily.

Later, during counselling in Chennai, he was advised to talk more and not treat it as a problem. He was also told about "stranger talk." At that time, he lived in Pallavaram and walked 2 km daily to practice talking to strangers.

Eventually, he decided it was a mistake to hide behind his stammer and live as an introvert. He resolved to speak for his life. Though he wanted to become an assistant director, financial burdens led him to work instead. After working for 3–4 years in system servicing and later in a non-voice BPO, he joined Dell in 2012. Working night shifts and sleeping daily made him feel like a machine. It forced him to reflect: "Are we going to live like this until we die?"

He quit the job with his father's consent and pursued his dream in cinema. With no industry connections, he joined a film shoot for 15 days. But realising the project was going nowhere, he quit, understanding that many such meaningless films exist in the industry.

Then, he searched for a well-known director to work under. Two years passed. At age 27, his father reminded him that he needed a job before they could look for a bride. Though Alphonse had sworn never to carry a file and attend interviews again, fate had other plans.

A turning point occurred—his uncle in Bengaluru asked him to meet a contact in Chennai, someone close to actor Rajinikanth. He met two people, one of whom was Ramesh (name changed) from Zee Tamil, who said, "I know many directors. Work with me for a while." Alphonse worked unpaid in Ramesh's spiritual travel agency for six months.

Later, Ramesh suggested he try photography for income, asking Alphonse to take orders and earn commissions. Though Alphonse knew nothing about photography, he pitched creatively and got a few small orders. Realising that Ramesh had no intention of helping him enter the film industry, Alphonse politely left and fulfilled the orders he had already taken.

He decided to pursue photography full-time. Thus, **Aliens Photography** was born in June 2014.

He started with a few visiting cards and an old tablet, stopping people on the road in the Parrys market area to secure wedding photography orders. He outsourced everything but ensured high quality. After two months, he got a small shop to work from, hired staff, and slowly built a stable income. When he asked his father how much money was needed for his wedding, his father said Rs. 4 lakhs. Alphonse replied, "I'll give three lakhs—you manage the rest." Within six months, he fulfilled that promise. His father was finally convinced that his son had made it in life.

In November 2017, Selvarani entered his life. During their arranged meeting, Alphonse spoke with her for 10 minutes but didn't mention his stammer. Through regular phone calls, she figured it out herself but never made it an issue. She later mortgaged her jewellery to help him buy a camera. He returned the money in a few months. Staff grew from 2 to 6; Aliens Photography has completed over 1400 weddings today. Clients recognise Alphonse personally, and he receives over 50 calls daily. His quality and sincerity have made him successful.

In April 2020, he joined TSS and remains active to this day. Those who attended SHG meetings at his office found him an inspiration. He never misses workshops and learns something new about stammering every time.

His father used to call him "overconfident," but Alphonse knows that confidence is what brought him this far. People who once mocked his career choice now praise him. He believes his stammer, inherited from his father, made him struggle, fight, and eventually succeed.

Today, he lives in Vadapalani, Chennai, with his wife and two children and runs a successful office.

In 2020, Alphonse spent ₹95,000 to direct a short film, proving to the world that a director still lives within him. The same dream he declared in school 15 years ago came full circle when classmates who once mocked him apologised and praised him on Facebook. That boosted his morale even more.

At age 37, he now works part-time as an Assistant Director under a well-known filmmaker while continuing to run his photography business. He strongly believes his beloved cinema will one day bring him major success.

Alphonse has stammered in countless interviews. Today, he conducts interviews for his own company. He still stammers, but he's moving forward, and his speech continues to improve.

"So, what if I stammer? I speak! What's wrong with that?"—This is the Alphonse of today.

The last salary he ever earned under someone else was ₹12,000. Today, even his junior staff earn more than that.

He says:

"Struggle in life. Otherwise, you'll end up living a dull existence. Be sincere and loyal to your job or business—it will always protect you."

S. Alphonse – Chennai - Tamil Nadu

Email: aliensphotographychennai@gmail.com

20

THE COURAGE TO BREAK THE BARRIERS

HIGH SCHOOL STRUGGLES AND ADAPTATION

After completing 10th grade, Supradeepan transferred to a nearby school for his higher secondary education. Initially, he was anxious about introducing himself in class. However, when he realised it wasn't mandatory, he felt relieved.

Yet, a new challenge arose during morning assemblies. Students were required to recite Thirukkural verses or read news headlines on stage. The fear of public speaking horrified him so much that he skipped school for three days. The anxiety of standing in front of a crowd deeply affected him, making him consider quitting school altogether.

Understanding his son's distress, his father spoke to the school principal, who exempted him from speaking at assemblies. This gave Supradeepan the confidence to refocus on academics. Despite his father's and speech therapist's efforts, the therapy showed limited improvement.

COLLEGE LIFE AND SELF-DISCOVERY

After high school, he pursued a B. Tech in Information Technology at Dr. M.G.R. Educational and Research Institute. Despite his stammering challenges, he enjoyed college life and developed a deep passion for IT-related subjects. His dedication and hard work earned him top rank in class. His professors were highly supportive, which helped him thrive academically.

A NEW IDENTITY: SAI SRIKANTH

During this time, he noticed that he could easily pronounce his friends' names but struggled with his name. He wondered if changing his name to something easier to pronounce might help. Since childhood, he has had a nickname: "Srikanth." Believing that a new name might help him manage his stammering better, he changed it legally. After discussing it with his parents, he officially adopted the name "Sai Srikanth," marking a new chapter in his journey.

JOB SEARCH STRUGGLES AND EARLY CAREER

After completing his undergraduate degree, Sai Srikanth faced significant job challenges. While he excelled in written and technical assessments, he struggled in interviews due to his stammering. The repeated failures shook his confidence, and the financial pressure at home forced him to take a KPO (Knowledge Process Outsourcing) job unrelated to his field of study.

SEEKING GROWTH DESPITE OBSTACLES

Over the next two years, he worked hard to advance his career. He applied for a team leader position and successfully cleared the written assessments. However, once again, his speech difficulties affected his interview performance, preventing him from securing the promotion.

A LIFE-CHANGING DISCOVERY – TAMIL SUPER SPEAKERS (TSS)

In May 2020, during the COVID-19 pandemic, Sai Srikanth came across the Tamil Super Speakers (TSS) Facebook group led by Mr. Manimaran. Soon, he received a life-changing call from Mr. Agni Raj, the Managing Director of the TSS group, who explained the root causes of stammering and practical strategies to manage it.

Following this, Sai Srikanth began daily speech practice. Initially, he practiced alone in a closed room. As his confidence grew, he started practicing openly at home without worrying about others' opinions.

BUILDING LEADERSHIP AND CONFIDENCE

Through Tamil Super Speakers, he connected with like-minded individuals, including Alphonse, and was encouraged to organise Self-Help Group (SHG) meetings in Chennai. These weekly Sunday meetings helped him improve his speaking abilities and leadership skills.

Participating in four speech therapy workshops and two All India Conferences organised by Tamil Super Speakers significantly boosted his confidence in public speaking. The next day, he felt a renewed enthusiasm to seize every opportunity to speak, embracing his journey with positivity and determination.

JOINING TOASTMASTERS AND ENHANCING COMMUNICATION SKILLS

After building a strong foundation in speech improvement, Sai Srikanth joined Toastmasters, an international platform that challenged him further and helped him grow alongside new members. The weekly opportunities at Toastmasters, combined with the skills he gained from Tamil Super Speakers, improved his fluency in speech and his English proficiency.

CAREER COMEBACK WITH RENEWED CONFIDENCE

Despite losing his job during the COVID-19 pandemic, Sai Srikanth did not lose hope. With his newfound confidence, he attended multiple interviews, significantly improving his communication skills. His perseverance paid off—he received job offers from three companies and finally secured a position in his dream IT field. He started working as a software tester at a private company in Chennai, where he now speaks more confidently than ever before.

LEADERSHIP AND PUBLIC RECOGNITION

A few years later, he was promoted to Team Leader, managing a group of eight members. In 2024, on International Stammering Awareness Day, he was invited as a guest RJ on Mirchi FM, where he shared his inspirational journey with a global audience.

SPREADING AWARENESS AND ENCOURAGING OTHERS

Reflecting on his journey, Sai Srikanth proudly states, *"Yes, I am a person who stammers, but I have overcome challenges through continuous effort!"*

He firmly believes that society is becoming more accepting of people who stammer. However, he also emphasises the need for greater awareness. Today, he is committed to raising awareness and inspiring others by sharing his story.

K. Sai Srikanth – Chennai - Tamil Nadu

Email: Saisrikanth.gunsekar@gmail.com

21

NOW BOLDLY DOING IT

M.R Prakash was born in 1973 in Palakkad, Kerala, into a middle-class family. He is the second of five children. From the time he started speaking, Prakash vividly remembers stammering. As he grew older, the stammering intensified.

THE SILENT STRUGGLES OF CHILDHOOD

Due to his speech difficulty, Prakash avoided speaking to anyone outside his home. An irrational fear always followed him, stemming from his stammering. He was a shy child from a young age—and that trait, although to a lesser extent, remains with him even today. Others often perceived him as a quiet, shy child. He recalls two unforgettable incidents from his school days.

The first happened when he was in the third grade. One day, a teacher named "Grace" asked him a few questions. Seeing him silent, she misinterpreted his behaviour and thought he was being arrogant. Believing he was refusing to answer out of pride, she scolded him. Only Prakash knew that his voice wouldn't come out due to his stammer. Deeply hurt, he burst into tears, ran home after school, and told his parents. His father immediately took him to the school and complained to the principal, who summoned the teacher. That's when she learned about his speech problem and apologised sincerely.

The second incident occurred in fifth grade. His Maths teacher would ask each student to stand in front of the class once a week and recite multiplication tables aloud. For Prakash, these moments felt like terrifying nightmares. When it was his turn, he would tremble with fear, trying to force out each number. He would hit his thighs and stomp his feet, giving the impression that he was dancing. Seeing this, the students laughed—and so did the teacher. This mockery felt like a thunderbolt to his tender heart.

In high school, despite knowing the answers, Prakash remained silent in class due to his stammer. Similarly, when asked to read aloud, he would stand and struggle immensely to utter the first word. Observing his struggle, teachers would tell him to sit down. He faced repeated humiliation from classmates. Even though he scored the highest marks in 10th grade, many teachers still didn't know his name because he had remained distant from both teachers and peers.

LAW SCHOOL AND LINGERING FEARS

College life wasn't much different. He had only a few friends. During those days, books were his best companion. He would head home immediately after classes. Due to his father's insistence, during his second year of undergraduate studies, he took the entrance exam for law school and secured admission to Thiruvananthapuram Law College.

Prakash joined law school hesitantly, knowing that good communication was vital for a lawyer. In his final year, before participating in "Moot Court" sessions, he took psychiatric medication for a few days to calm his mind and body. He graduated with a law degree in 1998.

After enrolling as a lawyer, he did not work for six months due to his fear of speaking. Again, encouraged by his father, he started working as a junior advocate while also preparing for government service exams.

In 2000, he secured a government job at a Panchayat office. However, new challenges awaited him. He struggled to interact naturally with colleagues and communicate effectively with higher officials. This created mental distress. He was so anxious about social situations that he wouldn't even touch the lunchbox he brought from home. Instead, he would eat alone in a hotel.

He feared participating in official meetings regarding staff transfers or retirements. He often made excuses and took leave during such sessions. Field inspections required by his job were also challenging. Attending departmental meetings and answering questions posed by superiors was particularly difficult. He realised that all these struggles stemmed from his stammering.

In 2002, he married Bindu. His stammering wasn't a barrier to getting married. His wife has never complained about his speech problem. She is a homemaker.

To overcome stammering, Prakash tried speech therapy, Ayurvedic and homoeopathic treatments, yoga, and meditation. None of these brought noticeable improvements. For a few years, to find temporary relief from stress and depression, he turned to alcohol and smoking. These unhealthy habits only weakened his mind and body further and worsened his stammering.

A TURNING POINT AT 47

When he was feeling hopeless, he happened to watch a speech practice video by Agnee Raj on YouTube. Soon, he joined the Tamil Super Speakers (TSS) group, created by Mr. V. Manimaran to support people who stammer. Prakash joined the group in 2020 at the age of 47.

Upon joining, he began doing the recommended one-hour daily speech practice every morning. Within three months, he noticed positive changes—his speech became clearer, and the frequency of stammering reduced. He actively participated in the group by posting voice recordings on daily topics and receiving support and encouragement from fellow members.

LEADERSHIP, LANGUAGE, AND LEGACY

After six months of speech practice, he gained the confidence to speak during office meetings. He, who once feared speaking about staff matters in meetings, began to speak boldly. Impressed by his enthusiasm and courage, Mr. Manimaran appointed him as the admin of the Malayalam Super Speakers group, which he continues to manage efficiently. Prakash records his speeches in meetings and posts them in the groups. These videos inspire others, motivating them to practice. Some Malayalam group members have made significant progress thanks to his support.

Prakash believes that openly accepting stammering and declaring, "Yes, I stammer," can ease mental pressure and help improve one's speech.

He started a YouTube channel and uploaded over 80 videos related to stammering. In July 2022, with the guidance of other admins, he successfully conducted a workshop for stammerers in his hometown of Palakkad.

He also translated Manimaran's English book *"S-S-Stammering"* into Malayalam. Without informing Prakash, Manimaran sent him ₹25,000 as a token of appreciation. However, Prakash returned the money and said he considered it a blessing to have done the translation, and that it was his small service to help Malayalam-speaking individuals who stammer. Such is Prakash's humility. Manimaran firmly believes that the Malayalam group is lucky to have Prakash as their admin.

LIVING PROOF THAT IT'S NEVER TOO LATE

Prakash has consistently practised speech for over four years. Now, he confidently speaks in all office meetings and even conducts some himself. Though he still stammers occasionally, he is no longer bothered by it. He leads a peaceful and happy life.

As mentioned earlier, his wife has always been supportive. Their only daughter, born in 2003, is currently in her fourth year studying to become an Ayurvedic doctor.

Although Prakash began his speech practice quite late, at the age of 47, he has no regrets. He firmly believes that young people who sincerely follow the TSS speech practices for three years will see remarkable improvements in their speech.

He acknowledges that his speech improvement is mainly due to the Tamil Super Speakers group, especially its core leaders, Mr Manimaran and Mr Agnee Raj, to whom he remains profoundly grateful.

M.R. Prakash – Palakkad - Kerala

Email: mrp9173@gmail.com

22

PERSEVERANCE & SUCCESS – "SELF–CONFIDENCE THAT COMES FROM MIMICRY"

Vijayamohan was born in 1980 into a middle-class family in the small town of Guduvanchery, near Chennai. Today, Guduvanchery has undergone rapid development and is now a big town. His father served in a senior position in the Tamil Nadu government and is now retired. His mother is a homemaker. He has only one younger sister.

One day, as a child, Vijayamohan ran out of his house, tripped, and fell. His teeth accidentally cut the tip of his tongue. His mother didn't realise the severity of the injury at first and applied coffee powder without checking correctly. His shirt was soaked in blood. Only then did she realise the seriousness and took him to a hospital, where doctors stitched his tongue with five sutures. Since then, he began stammering. No one else in his family had this issue.

Life in Guduvanchery was peaceful, but internally, a storm raged within him. After that incident, words felt like heavy stones stuck in his throat. Whenever he needed to speak, words would refuse to come out. Simple conversations became challenges. Reading aloud in class was a terrifying ordeal.

His parents didn't believe he had a stammering issue. They were convinced it was just fear and never took him to a doctor or offered any support for the problem.

In school, Vijayamohan was afraid to ask or answer questions. Sometimes, friends mocked his stammer. Going out to buy groceries or vegetables often turned into a humiliating experience. People looked at him as if he were from another planet and laughed. Rather than being broken by these experiences, he was determined to overcome them—and make those same people laugh at his talent.

He was inspired by the Tamil film comedian Chinni Jayanth's mimicry and deeply moved by Kamal Haasan's voice in the movie *Indian*. He began following Kamal Haasan and started mimicry as a hobby, which gradually turned into a talent.

Vijayamohan studied engineering at Sriram Engineering College, where he had a strong circle of supportive friends—Rajesh, Daya, Yadav, Murali, Pradeep, Palani, Ranga, and Senthil—who always stood by him. During a college cultural event, they encouraged him to showcase his mimicry. Though he hesitated at first, they suddenly thrown him onto the stage. With trembling hands, he delivered his first stage performance, which was a hit and received well. It became an unforgettable moment for him.

He recalls three particularly humiliating experiences:

1. Once, when buying a bus ticket, he couldn't say his destination. Everyone stared at him, and the conductor angrily yelled at him.

2. His manager once denied him a promotion, saying, "You're already struggling to complete your tasks due to your speech." How can we entrust you with leading a team?"

3. Due to intense stammering, he was unable to answer a question during a job interview. He was dismissed in 5 minutes and told he was unfit for the job.

There were also some funny moments. When he once claimed he could do good mimicry, his friends laughed and said, "You can't even talk properly—how can you mimic?" He surprised them by convincingly imitating Rajinikanth, Kamal Haasan, and Vijayakanth.

After several attempts, he got a job in the finance sector. He actively sought opportunities to speak onstage during office events and never let his speech problem hold him back. Due to his stammer, he often struggled with promotions or team leadership roles.

Determined to improve himself, he earned an MBA in 2005. During college, he participated in inter-college events and won many prizes. However, stammering still posed challenges. In campus interviews, although he excelled in written tests, he struggled during group discussions and final interviews. As a result, he was unable to secure a good job at that time.

In 2009, he married his cousin, who was already aware of his stammer. She has been highly supportive, especially when Vijay faced career setbacks due to his speech.

In 2018, determined to find a solution, Vijayamohan searched online and found Mr. Manimaran, helping people overcome stammering. Vijay contacted him and invited him to his home. Manimaran explained stammering, its causes, how to overcome it through speech practice, and why acceptance is essential. Vijay absorbed the techniques and practiced diligently, noticing improvement in his speech.

He used to actively attend self-help group meetings every Sunday at Anna Nagar Tower Park and regularly participate in Google Meet online sessions—sometimes even while driving. Manimaran later advised him not to join meetings while driving.

Vijayamohan's life took a turn when he entered sales and marketing in the banking sector, a role that required strong communication. Over time, he was promoted to a mid-management position, led large teams, and began speaking with confidence. Although he stammers occasionally, he learned not to let it affect his self-esteem.

Today, he works as a Cluster Manager in a well-known private bank. Now, he has two daughters who speak fluently.

He has performed over 60 mimicry shows and organised and hosted events both within and outside his company. At TSS workshops for people who stammer, his mimicry sessions are always a highlight. They are usually scheduled post-lunch when people tend to get drowsy. His humour wakes them up and energises the room. He never performs for money—only for noble causes. His spontaneous wit and natural humour have earned him a strong fan base.

Remarkably, even as a stammerer, he once appeared on Vijay TV's "Kalakka Povathu Yaaru", a popular Tamil comedy show.

About the Tamil Super Speakers (TSS) group, he says:

"TSS gave me hope. When I first met other stammerers like me, I realised I wasn't alone. The techniques, success stories, and testimonials convinced me I could overcome this. Speech practice gave me confidence."

Today, Vijayamohan stands as a symbol of courage and resilience. Despite stammering, he has excelled in sales, marketing, and mimicry and has captivated audiences through public speaking. His journey proves that any obstacle can be overcome with confidence, consistent practice, and perseverance.

His advice to young stammerers:

"Never give up. Be disciplined in your practice. Speak whenever you get the opportunity—don't let it pass. Most importantly, follow the guidance given by TSS without any doubts."

He concludes with a Tamil proverb:

"Sculptor and sculpture—we are both." Like the sculptor within us, the masterpiece also lies within us.

N. Vijayamohan – Chennai - Tamil Nadu

Email: vijayamohan0501@gmail.com

23

KOLAR TO MELBORNE

Udaya Kumar was born in 1989 in Kolar Gold Fields (KGF). His father worked in the Kolar Gold Fields and retired from service. His mother was a homemaker but is no longer alive. He has a younger brother and a younger sister. While his father was employed in Kolar Gold Fields, they lived as a middle-class family. However, when the gold fields were shut down in 2001, his father lost his job. That was when Udaya Kumar's family was pushed into poverty. His father struggled a lot to educate his children.

Until the age of ten, Udaya Kumar spoke fluently. However, his speech difficulty persisted due to the family's financial struggles and the lack of awareness about stuttering in the early 2000s.

Udaya Kumar studied at a school in Kolar Gold Fields. Due to his stammering, he was often isolated at school and in society. His classmates frequently mocked him and made fun of his speech, treating it as entertainment. The constant teasing led Udaya Kumar to withdraw from social interactions and develop a certain resentment toward the world.

Every day in the classroom, even saying "Present, Sir" during attendance was challenging for him. As he grew older, despite the teasing, he never considered his stammering a barrier. While pursuing engineering, Udaya Kumar faced numerous challenges.

He was given extra time during oral exams, which made him feel different from his peers. These experiences further shattered his confidence and made it even more difficult for him to cope with his speech impairment.

He pursued a degree in Mechanical Engineering at Chikkaballapur (Karnataka). Udaya Kumar completed his degree in 2011. As he entered the real world searching for a job, he faced the harsh challenge of job interviews. Due to his speech impediment, many companies rejected him. As the eldest son of a struggling family, he carried significant responsibilities. The pressure of speaking during crucial moments only increased his anxiety.

Eager to find a solution, Udaya Kumar searched online and discovered a stammering treatment centre in Bangalore. He underwent treatment there, but it did not yield the results he had hoped for. Eventually, he accepted his speech difficulty and secured a job at a company in Chennai, where he also got married and started his life.

One day, an opposing argument with a close friend brought back all his insecurities. A hurtful comment about his stammering and the deep sorrow of losing his mother triggered an emotional breakdown, making him doubt whether he would ever be able to speak fluently again. This severely affected his self-confidence and worsened his stammering.

Udaya Kumar's lifelong struggle with stammering remained an immense challenge. Since childhood, he had longed for a friend with whom he could speak freely. His speech impediment made social interactions difficult, and for 35 years, he had yearned to open his heart to someone. Yet, he still hoped that he would find a friend who truly understood him one day.

In search of another treatment option, he again turned to the internet. That's when he came across the Tamil Super Speakers group led by Mr. Manimaran.

Udaya Kumar contacted Mr. Manimaran and joined the Tamil Super Speakers WhatsApp group in September 2018. Later, in November 2018, he attended a workshop in Chennai specifically for people who stammer. There, he met many individuals facing the same challenges. For the first time, he realised that he was not alone—there were many others like him.

With guidance from senior WhatsApp group members and Mr. Manimaran, Udaya Kumar gradually began to accept his stammering openly. Once he embraced it, he started speaking more confidently. Even when he stammered, he did not hold back from speaking. After that, he worked hard and achieved remarkable success. Here are some of his accomplishments:

1. Winner of the 2019 International Innovation Competition

   * His innovative thinking and problem-solving skills were recognised on a global stage.

2. Ranked 5th in the Smart Up Challenge 2018

   * This international competition showcased his ability to compete with the best minds worldwide, representing India globally.

3. Received a Patent in 2019 for his Railway Sector Innovation

   * His unique design and innovation were officially recognised, proving his expertise and creativity in his field.

4. Won the Gold Medal at the Quality Circle Forum of India in 2022

   * This award recognised his commitment to continuous improvement and Kaizen innovation.

Udaya Kumar's journey from struggling with stammering to achieving international recognition is genuinely inspiring.

He transformed his biggest challenge into a stepping stone for success.

In April 2023, Udaya Kumar's life significantly changed when he received an international job opportunity. Despite initial fears, he faced the job interview confidently and secured the position. On April 16, 2023, he received his visa and moved to Melbourne, Australia, where he was appointed a specialist in Rolling Stock Car body in the Metro and Tram Manufacturing Industry.

Udaya Kumar's journey did not stop there. Even with his stammering, he successfully passed the IELTS/PTE exams. Additionally, in 2024, he obtained his Chartered Professional Engineer (CPEng) certification in Australia, further establishing his expertise in the field.

Funny Incidents Due to His Stuttering

Despite the challenges of stammering, Udaya Kumar had some amusing experiences. Here are three funny incidents:

1. The "Pineapple Pizza" Incident

    *   One day, Udaya Kumar tried to order a pepperoni pizza over the phone. However, his stammering made him say "Pi-Pi-Pineapple" instead of "Pepperoni." The person on the other end thought he wanted pineapple on his pizza and started laughing. Eventually, he received a pineapple pizza, which, surprisingly, turned out to be delicious!

2. The "What's My Name?" Interview Incident

    *   During a job interview in Bangalore, the interviewer asked for his name. Udaya Kumar struggled to say it due to his stammer. In frustration, he turned to his friend sitting beside him and asked, "Hey, what's my name?" The interviewer was shocked and

asked, "You don't know your name?" Though it was awkward, everyone had a good laugh about it later.

3. The "Wrong Destination" Auto Ride

  * In Chennai, Udaya Kumar tried to tell an auto driver to take him to "Central Bus Stand." However, he accidentally said "Ce-Ce-Central Park" instead due to his stammer. The auto driver misunderstood and took him to Central Park instead of the bus stand. Ultimately, Udaya Kumar enjoyed a nice walk in the park, turning the mishap into a fun experience.

Today, Udaya Kumar lives happily in Melbourne with his wife and their 5-year-old son. His journey from overcoming stammering to achieving international success is truly inspiring!

UDAYA KUMAR'S INSPIRING WORDS

"Even though my stammering has not been cured, I have learned to accept it. I realised that stammering is a part of me, but I did not let it define me. Instead, I learned to live with it. By doing so, I discovered freedom and self-acceptance."

Udaya Kumar's story stands as a testament to his resilience and determination. Despite facing numerous challenges, he never gave up and continued to strive for excellence. His achievements inspire countless individuals who stammer, proving that they, too, can overcome obstacles and achieve their dreams.

S. Udaya Kumar – Melbourne - Australia

Email: udayakumar.official1989@gmail.com

24

SALESMAN TURNED OWNER

My name is Rajesh Purohit. I was born into a humble family on May 17, 1991, in the Sirohi district of Rajasthan. My father worked in an iron factory, and my mother is a homemaker. I have one elder brother, one elder sister, and one younger sister. I have been a stammerer since childhood. My father also used to stammer, but improved with age. He now only stammers occasionally under stress.

My family has always been supportive of my stammering. They understood my feelings and the pain it caused me. But no one outside my family could truly understand what I went through.

I studied up to 8th grade in our village. During roll calls at school, I could not say "Present, sir" on time. Since our school required students to raise their hands while responding, I would only raise my hand, and my bench mate would say "Present" on my behalf. Teachers avoided asking me to speak due to my stammer.

My father moved to Chennai in 1980 and worked as a manager for 40 years in an iron factory. He worked hard and educated all four of his children. I later moved to Chennai with my family. I completed my schooling up to 12th grade in Chennai and then pursued B.Com through correspondence at the University of Madras. Since I didn't attend regular college, I avoided self-introductions, seminars, and presentations.

Though I was always good at my studies, I struggled with oral exams. I never asked questions or volunteered to speak. My fear worsened over time, and I became more withdrawn. I had very few friends. Simple tasks like grocery shopping, buying medicine, getting a bus ticket, talking in front of guests, or visiting someone's house were painful. I often felt like running away to someplace where no one could see me. I cried many times and questioned why God gave me this problem. Later, I told myself, "I can bear this. I am strong and won't lose courage." I had many dreams, and although I was afraid to speak, I could achieve some more slowly than others.

I faced severe emotional distress due to stammering. I will never forget one incident: One day, I went to book a train ticket. There was a long queue. When my turn came, I couldn't say the name of my destination. People behind me started shouting, and the ticket clerk yelled, "Move aside! Go to the back of the line!" That was a horrible day. I couldn't sleep all night. I began to think I would never achieve anything in life. Negative thoughts overwhelmed me.

When I joined Vivo Mobile as a salesperson, I introduced myself to the manager. When he asked my name, I couldn't say it. After observing my stammering, he kindly said, "Why did you choose sales? You have to communicate effectively here and explain things clearly to customers." I said, "Sir, I need a job." He hired me. I worked hard and consistently performed well. I was even rewarded for speaking, which further boosted my confidence.

I started calling many customer service centres to overcome my fear of talking to strangers. In May 2019, I got Mr. Manimaran's phone number. I immediately called him, and he invited me to visit him at his home on a Sunday.

When I met him, I liked his approach. He explained in detail what stammering is, how to overcome it, why speech practice is critical, how and how long to do it, and why we should accept stammering. He encouraged me to start practising my speech. Since he was helping selflessly and free of charge, I felt inspired and started practicing the techniques he taught. However, after a month, my stammering worsened. I called him again, and he reassured me: "That's normal initially. Don't stop—keep practising." So, I continued.

During this time, I attended two stammering workshops in Chennai. In December 2019, I participated in a workshop in Madurai, where I met Mr. Balasubramanian Ji, who had learned speech practice from Andrew Bell Sir. It was an unforgettable moment in my life. I also learned finer techniques from Balasubramanian Sir and Agnee Raj Sir.

After 200 days of speech practice, I had to return to my hometown in Rajasthan, so I temporarily paused my practice. Later, I returned to Chennai and resumed practicing. Gradually, I saw significant improvement. Seeing my progress, Manimaran Sir asked me to record a video in Hindi demonstrating the technique and upload it to his YouTube channel. I recorded it and sent it to him. Once uploaded, many Hindi-speaking individuals who stammered started connecting with us.

When these new members began their speech practice, they had many questions. I answered them. So far, over 2,000 people have watched my Hindi video. After 150 days of practice, many of them experienced improvements. Manimaran Sir and I started a Hindi WhatsApp group to guide more people. The group continued to grow, and I became a bridge for spreading this technique among Hindi speakers.

Today, more than 250 Hindi speakers regularly benefit from this practice. As I'm the only Hindi-speaking person who has personally met Balasubramanian Sir, Manimaran Sir, and Agnee Raj Sir, I had the opportunity to share these techniques with others. Teaching others also helped me learn more.

Since childhood, I have dreamed of working in a mobile phone company—and I achieved that. I have mastered all the skills required for mobile phone sales. I practised speech techniques for 500 days. I gained immense confidence. I still stammer, but I'm no longer embarrassed in public. My fear has dramatically reduced. Whether I stammer or not no longer matters to me. I practiced daily and uploaded voice recordings to our group. I improved steadily.

Then, in December 2023, I quit my job and opened my mobile phone and accessories store in Chennai. I still stammer, but I no longer focus on it. I have no fear. I've worked in my dream job and advanced to owning a mobile store myself.

I'm grateful to Manimaran Sir for teaching me speech techniques selflessly and transforming my life. I wish him a long, healthy life and hope this book's readers live confidently.

Rajesh. C Purohit – Chennai - Tamil Nadu

Email: raazraigur@gmail.com

25

LET'S LIVE BOLDLY

Boomesh was born in 1997 in Valayapalayam, located in the Thiruppur district. He is the only child of his uneducated parents, who work and live on someone else's farm. A few months after Boomesh was born, his father developed a mental illness and has since been unable to perform any work independently. His mother supports the family by taking on small chores on the farm.

Boomesh studied from grades 1 to 5 at a Panchayat Union Primary School in Valayapalayam, grades 6 to 10 at the government-aided NR Karuppanna Nadar School in Kunnathur, and grades 11 and 12 at Vairavilas Higher Secondary School, a government school in Gobi Chettipalayam. Since he studied in government schools, his entire schooling was free. His maternal uncle and a few relatives supported him with other minor expenses.

During school, Boomesh's stammering was minimal. He had no problem answering roll calls and wasn't even aware he had a stammer. Some teachers and classmates did mention that he stammered slightly. He was a good student and consistently ranked among the top 5 in class.

After completing school, Boomesh joined Gobi Arts and Science College to study B.Sc. in Physics (2013–2016), followed by an M.Sc. in Physics at the same college (2016–2018). Due to his family's poor financial situation, he started working part-time from the time he joined college. At night, he used to wash buses, earning ₹150 per bus. Washing three buses daily, he earned ₹450 a day, which he used to fund both his education and household expenses.

After completing his MSc, he pursued an MPhil at Chikkaiah Naicker College in Erode. After completing his M.Phil., he applied for a lecturer position and was called for an interview. Unfortunately, he stammered a lot during the interview. Although stammering had never previously caused him issues, it affected him this time. The interviewer rejected him, saying a stammering lecturer could not do the job effectively. At another college interview, he stammered again, but the interviewer was kind and offered him a job, advising him to work on his speech.

The salary was low, so he worked there for only eight months. He then attempted to work in the film industry in Chennai but disliked it and returned to his hometown after just three months. A friend suggested that he pursue a PhD immediately, explaining that it would be more challenging to do so later in life.

Taking that advice, Boomesh quit his job and enrolled in a PhD program at Ramakrishna Mission College in Coimbatore. He is expected to complete it in about six months.

About his PhD, Boomesh explains:

"Due to various accidents and natural causes, many cells and tissues in the human body are damaged. Instead of sourcing tissues from another person, it's possible to produce them synthetically. My research focuses on creating artificial tissues by chemically combining compounds using a method called plasma polymerisation. These artificial tissues are then tested in various experiments, and the results are to be published."

His PhD supervisor is very supportive and covers all research-related expenses, considering Boomesh's financial background.

It was during that first failed interview that Boomesh realised he had to overcome stammering. In 2019, while searching online, he came across a video by Agnee Raj Anna. In the video, Agnee Anna exposed individuals who claimed to cure stammering quickly for a fee and instead recommended the Tamil Super Speakers (TSS) group, which provides free support.

Inspired, Boomesh contacted AgneeRraj Anna and joined TSS. He learned speech techniques and participated in several workshops for people who stammer. One memorable workshop was at Agnee Raj Anna's son's school in Madurai, where Agnee Raj Anna gave an impactful speech:

"Friends, understand your stammering thoroughly before beginning your practice." Let people mock us—it doesn't matter. Those who mock us won't stay in our lives forever. Stop worrying about whether others will think you stammer. Speak boldly and continue your practice."

However, due to various reasons, Boomesh was unable to practice consistently beyond three months. This inconsistency prevented him from completely overcoming his stammer. But he has now resolved to practice daily and improve his speech before completing his PhD.

His current goal is to work abroad after completing his PhD. In Tamil Nadu, even PhD holders receive low pay as assistant professors, while research jobs abroad offer much better salaries. He has already started working towards this plan and is expected to complete his PhD and secure a job abroad by the end of 2025. The TSS group extends its best wishes to him.

Even while pursuing his PhD, Boomesh has continued to work part-time. He still washes one bus per night, earning ₹150 daily. When Mr. Manimaran asked how he managed his finances, Boomesh explained that his parents had sold a piece of their land and deposited the money in a bank. They now live off the interest from that deposit. Boomesh stays in a shared room with friends in Coimbatore, while his parents live in a small house on the farm. He visits them once a week.

BOOMESH'S ADVICE TO OTHERS WHO STAMMER

"If someone consistently practices the techniques taught by the TSS group—daily speeches on given topics, stranger talk, self-help group meetings, and Google Meet sessions—for at least six months, anyone can recover 75% of their stammering. Even if he stops after six months, you can restart later."

V. Boomesh – Thiruppur - Tamil Nadu

Email: vellingriiv209@gmail.com

26

HUMILIATION IS THE FIRST STEP TOWARDS PROGRESS

My name is V. Yuvaraj. I was born in Chennai in 1999. My father is an auto driver, and my mother is a homemaker. I have an elder brother who is seven years older than I am. My family was impoverished, and because of this, I became aware of financial struggles from a very young age.

REALISING MY STAMMERING ISSUE

I first realised that I had a stammer in the 5th grade when I was asked to read a passage aloud in front of the teacher. I struggled to read fluently. I studied at that school until the 8th grade. Every Friday, the teachers conducted prayer meetings for me. They consoled me and confidently said that my stammering would be cured one day.

Like most people who stammer, I faced many difficulties during school.

* Roll call was always challenging because I had trouble saying "Present, sir" smoothly.

* Even though I was a good student, I avoided answering teachers' questions out of fear of stammering—even when I knew the correct answers.

* Because of this, I got scolded and even punished physically many times.

A HEARTBREAKING INCIDENT

One year, during the Christmas celebrations at school, a play was organised. The play had many king roles, and I was selected to play a king. I was excited, and they even placed a crown on my head for the role. However, another teacher noticed me and said, "This boy can't speak properly. He will stammer while talking. He should not act in this play."

After hearing that, the teachers changed my role. Instead of playing the king, I was made to stand behind the king as a silent character, without a single dialogue. The moment I should have proudly played a king; I was pushed to the background. This deeply hurt me and left me feeling humiliated.

DREAMS AND NIGHTMARES

Every night, I had many dreams. I dreamt that I was speaking fluently—either on a stage or in a public place. But along with those dreams, I also had dark thoughts:

* "Why was I born like this?"

* "I don't like this life."

* "God, please take me away."

These thoughts haunted me every single night in different ways.

COLLEGE LIFE – A TURNING POINT

I pursued my BSc in Zoology at Presidency College, Chennai, one of the most prestigious and oldest state colleges. My college years were both a period of fear and happiness. Why?

Because college taught me valuable life lessons about love, communication, learning, and many other things, I even earned the title "Jolly Person" among my friends.

OVERCOMING MY STAMMER IN COLLEGE.

Surprisingly, most people in college never knew that I had a stammering issue. No one asked me about it, and I never spoke about it. However, I had to speak more frequently when I became a student leader. This forced me to break out of my shell, and my low self-esteem was reduced by half.

POST-COLLEGE STRUGGLES

After graduating, a huge reality check awaited me at home. Our poverty had reached its peak. My elder brother got married and could no longer provide financial support. One day, he told me:

"From now on, you must take care of our parents."

That terrified me. I had to succeed—at any cost—to give my parents the happiness they never had. But getting a job was a nightmare. I faced endless rejections and failures in job interviews.

Why?

Because of my stammer, many companies refused to hire me.

STRUGGLING TO SURVIVE

During that phase, I did many jobs that people couldn't imagine.

* Even in 8th grade, I worked in a printing press.

* After college, I worked as a janitor in a hostel, cleaning floors, fans, and bathrooms.

* Later, I worked in catering services.

* I served food and even cleared used banana leaves after meals.

* I also worked as a cook.

STRUGGLES AND ODD JOBS

At one point, I worked in a wholesale market selling pins and clips. For a few days, I worked in a medical shop. Later, I worked as a salesman at Pantaloons in Express Avenue Mall. I also worked in a shoe store. Then, I did delivery jobs for Amazon, Swiggy, Zomato, and Dunzo.

After that, I tried my hand at medical coding. At one point, I worked for a lawyer, collecting legal documents. I also worked in a pen shop in Sowcarpet. For a while, I was distributing cigarettes. I even worked as a house-moving labourer, shifting household items from one home to another. That job broke me. I cried a lot while doing it because the items were so heavy.

Through all these jobs, I was doing just one thing. Trying to lift my family out of poverty.

A TURNING POINT – JOINING THE TSS GROUP

While desperately searching for a good job, I was introduced to Mr. Manimaran and Agnee brother, who ran the TSS Group. That group—and the families in it—became a turning point in my life. It was not just a group for me. I considered every single member as my own family. Why?

Because of this group, miracles and transformations started happening in my life. I could talk about every member individually because each person helped me differently.

LESSONS FROM THE TSS GROUP

Through this group, I learned:

* Speech therapy

* Breathing exercises

* Personality development

* The power of human thoughts

I was determined to make an impact in the group. So, I actively participated in:

* Speech recordings for every topic

* Tasks and activities given to us

I consistently practiced speech therapy for two years. Even today, the impact of that training is deep within me. I learned how to speak confidently on stage and present myself in the media—all because of this group.

THE ROLE OF MR. MANIMARAN IN MY JOURNEY

Mr. Manimaran has played a key role in my journey. Whenever I have doubts about public speaking, office life, or personal life, I immediately go to his house, ask questions, and get clarity.

BEFORE & AFTER JOINING THE TSS GROUP

I can divide my life into two parts:

Before joining the TSS group and after joining it.

BEFORE JOINING THE GROUP

* If someone mocked me, I would get furious.

* I would fight with them.

* Sometimes, I even got into physical fights.

* Back then, I had no idea about "Acceptance."

* I never thought about accepting my stammering.

AFTER JOINING THE TSS GROUP

* I learned about Acceptance.

✳ I told myself, "So what if I stammer? This is how I talk! If you want to listen. Listen! If not, walk away!"

✳ I actively participated in all activities for three years.

✳ I conducted online meetings and SGH meetings.

✳ I sometimes even took up the group's admin role for one day.

✳ Whenever I got to speak, I faced it with courage.

On August 15, during the Tambaram workshop, I did something for the first time: I spoke in front of a microphone. That day, I felt a sense of true freedom. I immediately posted about it on WhatsApp, Facebook, and Instagram: "Today, I have achieved real independence!"

THE POWER OF ACCEPTANCE

People who once said, "You can never speak properly!". Now, telling me,

"Dude, can you stop talking for a while?". That transformation happened because of one thing.

ACCEPTANCE of my stammering.

This acceptance has helped me grow in stammering and various aspects of life. Today, I even advise others on different matters. Now, if someone asks about me, they say: "He's an excellent speaker! A funny guy! He can mesmerise people with his words!"

A CAREER SHIFT FOR GROWTH

I got into a well-known software company with the help of my sister-in-law. However, I decided to change my job for three main reasons:

Comfort Zone – Staying in the same company for over 3-4 years creates a comfort zone.

Proving Myself – I wanted to prove to those who doubted me by securing a better position elsewhere.

Learning & Growth – I wanted to gain more experience in different areas.

For my career growth, I have now moved to a banking job. The work is entirely sales-related, and it is a field job that requires me to be on the move and talk more.

MY ADVICE TO FELLOW STAMMERERS.

I am not old enough or experienced enough to give big advice to others. I am still growing in my journey. However, at the insistence of Manimaran Sir, I am sharing a small piece of advice from my experience.

"Stammering is not a big problem—there are far more essential things in life. We should keep running toward our career goals and continue working on our stammering. If you stay in this group for two or three years, you will deeply understand stammering. Once you truly understand it, you won't feel bad about it, even if you stammer. That is the real secret of overcoming stammering!"

V. Yuvaraj – Chennai - Tamil Nadu

Email: yuvarajvns@gmail.com

27

THORNS & FLOWERS ON MY JOURNEY

Prabin was born in May 1992 in Mayilakodu, a village in the Kanyakumari district, where the three seas meet. He is the eldest child in his family, with a younger brother and sister. As a young child, he was energetic and loved playing with other kids, enjoying their company immensely.

His father was a construction worker. In kindergarten, Prabin was cheerful, participating in singing and speech competitions and winning prizes. He was also a bright student.

In 4th grade, Prabin experienced a life-changing moment. A teacher asked him to read aloud in class. He stood up, but no words came out. He stammered, and his classmates laughed—including his friends. Tears rolled down his cheeks. That day, Prabin first realised he had a speech disorder: stammering.

Just like being haunted by a ghost, stammering made it impossible for him to be at peace. He began distancing himself from friends. Though he longed to be with them, their teasing pushed him into solitude. He started hating school.

As time went on, his stammering worsened. From children to adults, everyone questioned him: "Why do you speak like that?" These constant remarks hurt him deeply. He would cry to his grandmother. Full of affection, she tried home remedies like applying herbal pastes on his tongue—but nothing worked. She comforted him, saying, "Your father used to stammer too, but it got better. Don't worry."

That same year, his father passed away. Due to poverty, his mother began working, and Prabin was sent to a hostel in the 5th grade. He pleaded, "Please don't leave me there—I can't speak well!" But fate had its way.

New school, hostel life, loneliness, stammering, fear, sadness—all kinds of negative emotions surrounded him. During roll calls, when he tried to say "Present, sir," the class would laugh. The pain grew each day. He longed to speak in class and participate in speech competitions, but his stammer held him back.

He began hating himself. He thought even his family disliked him because of his speech, so he was sent to the hostel. In 5th grade, he attempted to escape. He climbed a wall and walked 15 kilometres back home, not knowing the route correctly.

Only after reaching home did he realise the family's harsh poverty. They didn't dislike him—they couldn't afford otherwise. He understood and was sent to another hostel. He spent 8 years in a hostel 35 kilometres from home.

He studied at a reputed all-boys school in Kanyakumari, which gave him some peace. Still, his stammering made daily life difficult. He couldn't buy bus tickets or order food unless it was something he could say fluently. Often, he would order dishes he disliked to speak without stammering.

Teachers would ask questions to which he knew the answers, but rather than face the laughter from stammering, he would say, "I don't know," and get scolded or hit. Each scolding broke his spirit.

While others played, he would walk to the nearby church, praying and crying to God. He had no friends, no relatives to open up to. His only comfort came from two things—books and God. He spent more nights sleeping with books than in his mother's lap. He even contemplated suicide several times, and only books talked him out of it.

He wanted to join the NCC (National Cadet Corps), but the master said, "You stammer—you can't join." Time passed, and the "monster" of stammering grew inside him. Making phone calls became a nightmare. Since his home didn't have a phone, he had to call his mother at her workplace or a neighbour's home—but talking to strangers first terrified him, so he avoided calls altogether.

When others in the hostel called home for their needs, Prabin wouldn't. If he needed a notebook, he would collect old paper and boxes and sell them to a junk shop to buy what he needed. He wept while gathering those items because stammering had forced him into such situations.

After school, he joined a Diploma in Mechanical Engineering, choosing that stream only because his friend said, "No girls will join it," making life a little easier.

In college, no one mocked him. Partly because Prabin was 6 feet tall and looked physically strong due to gym workouts, many would stare at him, silently wondering if he stammered. Though dark-skinned, he was confident in his looks.

But as college ended, fear and anxiety returned— "How will I attend interviews? I must get a job soon—I'm the eldest son." He graduated in 2013.

He attended several interviews. When asked his name, he stammered, "P-P-Prabin," and got rejected. In one interview, the interviewer yelled, "Who let you in? You expect me to waste time interviewing someone like you?" That public humiliation shattered him, and he began withdrawing from everyone.

He became afraid to leave the house. Repeatedly, he said, "My education was useless. No one will ever hire me." Though the eldest son, he retreated into himself, helpless and dependent.

Every day, he cried. "My mother worked hard to educate me, and I've failed. I can't even speak. I don't deserve to eat." He felt utterly worthless. "Why did God create me like this?" he would cry often.

Eventually, his younger brother began working to support the family, and people mocked him: "Your younger brother works while you sit at home!" These words crushed him further.

Years after graduation, Prabin began working as an electrician in his village. In 2020, while searching YouTube for "stammering cure," he found videos by Mr. Agnee Raj, and everything changed.

He says:

"I had watched many stammering videos, but what struck me was Agnee brother's interviewing strangers about what they thought of people who stammer. It was eye-opening. I watched every video on the *Stammering Tamil* YouTube channel. They were amazing.

I messaged him on WhatsApp, and he called me directly. I thought it was a business gimmick, and he'd ask for a big fee. But he patiently spoke with me for 90 minutes, clearly explaining what stammering is, why it happens, and how to overcome it.

He said, "You don't need to pay anything. Join the group and practice." He couldn't believe it!

A week prior, Prabin consulted a doctor who said, "You have stage 4 stammering." You'll need expensive therapy sessions—and even then, only limited improvement." So, hearing that help was free stunned him.

Agnee brother added him to the Tamil Super Speakers (TSS) group, led by Mr. Manimaran, the group's chairman. For someone who had struggled alone for years, TSS gave Prabin hope and a new life.

Reading other members' stories made him realise that stammering is not a barrier to success.

His mental barriers shattered within days. He practiced daily using TSS techniques, and within 3–4 months, he could pronounce many words fluently. His confidence soared.

In late 2020, he attended a mini TSS workshop in Madurai and again in 2021, for a two-day workshop at Tiruchirappalli. There, he not only learned about stammering but also got to speak on stage with a mic—a childhood dream fulfilled. The tears he once shed in frustration now flowed in joy.

Using the confidence from the workshop, he later spoke in front of 800 people in his village. It was a proud moment—proof that he had conquered his fear.

He even went to an interview in Delhi, where a British interviewer spoke with him for 20 minutes. Prabin calmly and confidently answered everything, and he got selected.

Today, he works in Saudi Arabia at the world-renowned Almarai, a food company owned by the Royal family and managed by a British administration. When he flew there, he felt like a butterfly soaring free, no longer imprisoned by stammering.

Although he still stammers a little, he laughs more and confidently tackles work challenges. He interacts with people from many countries daily in person and via calls. And he still practices speech exercises for 30 minutes every day. TSS topics keep him inspired.

He deeply thanks Mr. Manimaran, Agnee Raj Anna, and all TSS members. Reading the book *"Stammering"* by Mr. Manimaran gave him deep insights into accepting stammering and practicing speech mindfully.

He ends with thanks to:

* His mother, who longed to hear him speak fluently

* His grandmother was his support during challenging times

* His siblings, who never gave up on him

* His friends and well-wishers who stood by him

"Let us set aside all differences and live joyfully on the path of love."

M. Prabin – Nagercoil – Saudi Arabia

Email: prabinm81@gmail.com

28

STAMMERING IS NOT A BARRIER TO DOING SOCIAL SERVICES

Manikandan was born in 1985 in Purasawalkam, Chennai. His father worked as a postman, and his mother was a homemaker. Manikandan is the eldest in his family and has a younger brother. He has been a person who stammers since birth. Interestingly, his father also used to stammer, but he eventually spoke fluently through persistent speech practice (even talking with pebbles in his mouth). His father passed away in 2022.

During his school and college days, Manikandan faced the same struggles and pain that many stammer experienced. He couldn't say "Present, sir" during the roll call. Even when he knew the answers to the teacher's questions, fear would make him say, "I don't know." He would never raise doubts or questions in class.

College life was no different—it was filled with shame and humiliation. He pursued a Diploma in Mechanical Engineering (DME) from CMJ University in Meghalaya. Throughout his studies, he experienced many embarrassing situations. He couldn't say his name correctly, tell the name of his destination on a bus, or order his favourite food in a restaurant. If he could say the name of a dish he disliked without stammering, he would order that to avoid the struggle. He couldn't say his parents' names fluently. Asking for directions or telling someone his phone number was always a major challenge.

His parents took him to several doctors to find a cure. At age 15, a doctor suggested that his enlarged tongue was the cause and recommended surgery. The surgery was done, but there was no improvement. At age 24, another doctor again suggested tongue surgery, and he went through a second procedure, still no improvement. Yet another doctor advised him to twist and train his tongue—but that too brought no change.

After completing his DME, he worked in a few companies. He also tried to get married, but all prospective brides rejected him due to his stammering.

His grandfather was an astrologer, and Manikandan chose to follow this ancestral profession. Despite his stammering, he is also a social worker. Whenever he saw a public issue, he would resolve it himself.

One such issue was the neglected temple pond at Arulmigu Gangadhareswarar Temple in Purasawalkam, Chennai, a historic Shiva temple representing the water element among the Pancha Bhootha Sthalams. For many years, the temple tank remained in disrepair. In 2019, he brought the issue to the attention of the former MLA and the senior officials of the Hindu Religious and Charitable Endowments (HR&CE) Department. Despite multiple petitions and letters, no action was taken.

So, Manikandan met the then HR&CE Commissioner in person and submitted a petition. With continued efforts and the support of TV and print media friends, he pushed the restoration initiative forward. Eventually, the HR&CE Minister visited the site and ordered restoration, and the tank was finally renovated in 2023 by the Tamil Nadu Government. The pond holds water again, and a Kumbhabhishekam was also performed that year.

Despite stammering, Manikandan boldly gave interviews on many news channels, advocating for public causes. He stands as a role model for many who think, "If I can't fix my own problem, how can I help others?" Manikandan encourages all people who stammer to engage in public issues—doing so not only builds confidence but also helps solve real-world problems. *Two mangoes with one stone,* he says.

In 2021, while searching YouTube for ways to overcome stammering, he came across Mr. Agnee Raj and contacted him. That's how he joined the Tamil Super Speakers (TSS) group.

Mr. Manimaran and Mr. Agnee Raj of TSS cleared all his doubts about stammering and taught him a simple but effective daily speech practice. They advised him to do it every morning for an hour. Manikandan followed this diligently for 1,000 days.

He also participated in several TSS workshops and overcame his fear of public speaking by speaking on stage with a microphone. Both mentors shared this knowledge freely, without expecting money or reward, because they had been stammerers themselves. Like only a woman can truly understand another woman's heart, only a person who stammers can genuinely understand another stammerer's mental state.

Now, Manikandan has recovered 80% from his stammering. His mentor, Dr. Kaniyar A.N. Rajasekaran from Tiruppur, allowed him to speak about astrology on Puthuyugam TV twice. Manikandan is also being encouraged to speak at major astrology conferences.

He says that TSS is the key reason for all this progress. If one follows the speech practices shared in the TSS group daily, recovery from stammering is possible. He sincerely believes that everyone who stammers should consistently practice speaking and break free from stammering.

S. Manikandan – Chennai - Tamil Nadu

Email: purasaimani@gmail.com

29

A JOURNEY TOWARDS HOPE & FREEDOM

Sarathbabu, born in 1989 in Mahabalipuram, Tamil Nadu and grew up there. He has a brother and a sister. From a young age, he had a speech impediment. His father also had a speech impediment in his early years, but started speaking clearly as he grew older. Now, his father speaks very well.

When Sarathbabu was in the second grade, his teacher allowed him to act in a play called "Kattabomman." He was asked to play the role of Jackson Durai, a British officer who spoke with a stammer. Since Jackson Durai spoke with a stammer in Tamil, Sarathbabu was chosen for the role because he, too, had a stammer. This incident had a profound impact on Sarathbabu. It was then that he realised for the first time that he was a person who stammers.

The following year, Sarathbabu was again invited to participate in the school's annual event. This time, he was supposed to play a character that required him to speak fluently. During the rehearsal, he struggled to communicate clearly because of his speech issue, and eventually, the opportunity to play that role was taken away from him. This deeply saddened him, and the event solidified the thought in his mind that he was a person who stammers.

Despite his speech difficulty, Sarathbabu excelled in his studies, always being the top student in his class. All his teachers liked and supported him, making him proud. Whenever he stammered, his parents would help by conveying his message to others, always offering support. He completed his studies like this till the 10th grade.

An essential aspect of Sarathbabu's early school life was his courage. Up until the 8th grade, he actively participated in class discussions. Even though he stammered, he would ask questions to the teacher in front of his classmates.

Not only that, but he also answered questions with courage. Everything changed when he reached the 9th grade. From the 9th grade onwards, boys and girls had to study together in that school. Sarathbabu did not want to stammer in front of the girls. He felt embarrassed when they saw him speaking that way. Struggling with his speech, he began avoiding speaking out in class. When he stopped speaking up alone, his stammering got worse every time he tried to speak. As this situation worsened, his class teachers stopped encouraging him to read aloud or ask questions.

In the 11th grade, Sarathbabu faced a considerable challenge. Unaware of his speech impediment, his Tamil teacher asked him to deliver a lesson from the Tamil textbook in front of the class. Since Sarathbabu was the top student in the class, the teacher believed he could do it well. The teacher gave him a week to prepare for the speech. However, when the day arrived, Sarathbabu was so scared and tense that he refused to give the speech. Without understanding the reason for his hesitation, the teacher scolded him. Unable to handle the pressure, Sarathbabu covered his face with the book, broke down in tears, and sobbed uncontrollably. Seeing this, the teacher asked him to leave. Later, the other students spoke to the teacher about Sarathbabu's speech problem. During the break, the teacher apologised to Sarathbabu and advised him to manage his stammering problem.

Another incident took place when Sarathbabu was in his third year of college. One day, he met his sister's friend while returning home with his friend. When the girl saw Sarathbabu, she asked which college he had studied. No matter how hard Sarathbabu tried, he couldn't say the name of his college. The girl's expression changed. It was Sarathbabu's friend who answered her question. At that moment, Sarathbabu felt very bad about himself.

After completing his college education, Sarathbabu joined an IT company in 2014. Even at his workplace, his stammering continued. While participating in all events with his friends, he rarely spoke to others. Sarathbabu's friends understood this and always supported him whenever he stammered. He worked in that company until 2019.

In the meantime, Sarathbabu got married in 2018. His wife accepted his stammering and provided immense support, which she continues to provide even today. Whenever Sarathbabu faces difficulty speaking in public, his wife helps by speaking on his behalf.

In 2020, Sarathbabu joined another prestigious company. Through hard work and perseverance, he consistently received promotions. He is currently working as a senior manager. Although he faces many challenges when interacting with his team and colleagues daily, he remains focused on his responsibilities. Despite his stammering issue, he continues to complete his work efficiently.

The thought of overcoming his speech issue had always lingered in Sarathbabu's mind. While searching online, he discovered a group called *Tamil Super Speakers* (TSS), which helps with stammering problems. Sarathbabu joined this group on January 16, 2023. The group operates under the leadership of Mr. Manimaran and Managing Director Agni Raj Anna. They both taught Sarathbabu unique speech therapy he had never encountered before. They also advised him to participate in the group's daily activities actively. All of this was provided free of charge; not a single penny was charged.

The two most important lessons they taught were wholeheartedly accepting stammering and openly discussing it with others. From a young age, Sarath Babu never accepted his stammering. He hated it when he stammered and felt terrible about it. Over time, this hatred grew and became a deep emotional wound in his subconscious.

After joining the Tamil Super Speakers group, Sarath Babu experienced a significant shift in his mindset regarding his stammer. Until then, he had no clear understanding of how to manage it. He believed there was no solution to his speech problem and that it would remain a permanent part of his life.

The Tamil Super Speakers group completely transformed Sarath Babu. For the first time, he learned what stammering was and how to approach it positively. The group primarily emphasised speech practice. Secondly, as previously mentioned, it taught him to accept his stammer fully. Accepting it brought about a substantial mental shift and a sense of peace—even while stammering.

Sarath Babu also participated in the All-India Conference (AIC) for people who stammer in Yelagiri and a workshop held in Madurai. He interacted with many people who stammered and some who had overcome it. Through these conversations, he gained a wealth of knowledge about stammering. That was when he truly understood stammering in its entirety. Attending those two events provided him with valuable information and instilled in him the belief that it was possible to recover from it.

Sarath Babu firmly believes that if he continues practising speech therapy for two or three years and actively participates in the daily activities assigned by the group, he can reduce his stammering by 99%.

This newfound confidence had a positive impact on his professional life. Previously, if he had an episode of severe stammering, it would linger in his mind for a long time. But now, that's no longer the case. Even when he stammers, he moves past it quickly. He is now able to focus entirely on his work.

Sarath Babu understood how crucial good communication was for advancing in his career. Keeping that realisation in mind, he diligently practices his speech therapy daily. He firmly believes that he will be able to speak fluently in three years. He wholeheartedly appreciates the Tamil Super Speakers group for making this possible.

Sarath Babu's life is filled with happiness and peace—he has a loving wife and two beautiful sons.

He knows this is a long and challenging journey, but deep within, he believes that one day, he will completely overcome his stammer and speak fluently. He envisions a bright future and remains grateful to everyone who has helped him progress.

Sarath Babu shares a message for those who stutter through a short story:

"Stammering is not just a speech issue; it's also a personality challenge. Let me tell you a small story."

One day, three strangers happened to come to a hotel for breakfast. They didn't know each other, but they had one thing in common—they were all stammerers. All three of them wanted to eat Idlies. It was a self-service restaurant where customers had to stand in line, pay, and collect food.

The first person approached the counter, smiled at the staff, and said, "E-e-e... I want... I-I-Idly." His speech was not fluent, but the staff understood his request and gave him Idly. He happily sat down and enjoyed his breakfast. He stammered, but he wasn't worried about it. He wanted Idly, somehow managed to ask for it, and got what he wanted.

While standing in line, the second person started having negative thoughts run through his mind: *What if I stammer? What if the staff laughs at me?* At the last moment, he changed his mind and asked for Pongal instead of Idly, which he could say without stammering. He ate the Pongal, but every bite reminded him that he had not ordered what he truly wanted. The Pongal tasted fine, but his heart longed for Idly.

And the third person? He was so afraid of standing in line that he left without eating. The thought of speaking in front of strangers and fearing stammering made him walk away. He returned home, still hungry.

THESE THREE PEOPLE MADE THREE DIFFERENT CHOICES

* The first person faced his stammer, got what he wanted, and ate happily.

* The second person avoided stammering, but in doing so, he also avoided happiness.

* The third person avoided everything—speaking, people, experiences—and shrank his world.

Even if you stammer, be like the first person. Speak up even with a stammer, ask for what you want, and live your life to the fullest.

The goal is not perfect fluency. The goal is freedom to speak, stammer, laugh, and live without fear.

The next time you stammer, don't assume that people are judging you negatively. Most people don't know how to respond in that moment. Instead, they look to you for guidance.

Always remember this:

"How people see you depends on how you see yourself."

S. Sarathbabu – Chennai - Tamil Nadu

Email – samisarathbe@gmail.com

30

THE FEAR OF NOT FACING IS THE OBSTACLE TO STAMMERING

EARLY DAYS

Harish was born in 1997 in Rasipuram, Namakkal district, Tamil Nadu. He is his parents' only child and has been stammering since early childhood, much like his grandfather.

At age 9, during his school years, Harish was advised to participate in a Tamil speech competition to help him overcome fear and speak fluently. He registered, practiced at home, and prepared well. But on the day of the competition, standing before 10–12 students and the judges, he experienced overwhelming nervousness—sweaty palms, a tight throat—and he couldn't utter a single word despite trying many times. He stepped down in silence.

That moment left him humiliated and in tears. Deep inside, it had a lasting emotional impact. He began to believe that he would never speak fluently, unlike his friends, teachers, and family members.

A GROWING STRUGGLE

Harish began avoiding conversations with friends, family, and strangers as time passed. Outwardly quiet but inwardly restless, he became overly cautious about what and how to speak and constantly overanalysed every situation. Avoiding speech made his stammer worse. He couldn't understand why this invisible block kept stopping him.

This confusion and unpredictability made him feel ashamed and guilty for something that wasn't his fault. He wasn't choosing to stammer—it was just happening.

He couldn't express his feelings, say what he wanted, or even understand his emotions. Eventually, he began losing himself, which impacted his mental health. Even though his grandfather also stammers, Harish never found the courage to talk to him—or anyone else in the family—about his problem.

A FRUSTRATING START TO THERAPY

When he was 10, his mother took him to a speech therapist in Salem during a school vacation. The therapist asked him to say phrases, read newspapers aloud, and repeat particular articles. But Harish didn't understand the actual problem or purpose of those exercises. The pressure of these routines made things worse. Meanwhile, seeing his peers talk happily while he struggled made him even more upset.

Despite all these challenges, Harish excelled in school and college. Teachers saw him as a bright student. Studying helped him forget his speech issues, and education became his only hope for success. It gave him a sense of purpose and confidence.

ACADEMIC SUCCESS

Harish scored 93.8% in his 10th grade, 90.75% in 12th, and a 196.25/200 engineering cutoff score. These achievements helped him believe he could rise above stammering and succeed.

Through engineering counselling, he secured admission to the Petroleum Engineering program at Anna University, Chennai, in 2014. He enjoyed the early days of college, making new friends in a new city, but the happiness didn't last long.

At the end of each semester, he had to speak to the bank manager for education loan approval and present seminars in class. Each time, the stammering cycle returned. He struggled mainly when saying his name—Harish. There were four Harishes in his class; he was the third in alphabetical order. The first two were top students and very obedient. Harish was academically good, too, but not overly obedient like the others.

THE LAB RECORD INCIDENT

One day, he lost his Electrical Engineering lab record. Too lazy to rewrite all the experiments, he had a junior write it with help from his hostel friends. The junior returned the notebook a day before the exam.

But Harish was terrified—what if the exam instructor noticed that his handwriting didn't match? What if they asked questions he couldn't answer? Harish feared he might get caught and couldn't lie or explain due to his stammer.

On the exam day, the examiner was extremely strict, yelling at everyone. Harish nervously presented his observation sheet and lab record. The examiner signed the observation sheet and then opened the lab record.

As he opened it, he asked Harish his name. Harish said it slowly, without stammering. Then, the examiner asked, "Did you come to my room last week to meet me?" Though confused, Harish said, "Yes." The teacher smiled and praised him, calling him a sincere, disciplined student.

It then hit him—the examiner had confused him with another Harish, the top student. What he feared most turned out to be a funny and happy memory. That night, Harish reflected and laughed at how seriously he had feared a harmless situation.

College Final Year and Job Hunt

In the final year, two significant challenges awaited:

1. Project Viva – Harish couldn't say a single word during it. The shame of not being able to speak something he knew haunted him for days.

2. Campus interviews—2018 Harish began preparing but struggled in every interview. In 2019, he got a job as a chemical engineer in a small firm, but his stammer still bothered him.

During a five-day online meeting with managers and clients, Harish explained key project processes. He stammered heavily, but fortunately, his managers and directors focused on his skills, not his speech.

Still, the mental strain remained. He began attending interviews again for better jobs. Despite knowing all the answers, he failed repeatedly due to stammering. Over time, his confidence eroded. He began to hate himself for not being able to speak clearly and couldn't understand why.

Every time he walked out of an interview, he would recall Rajinikanth's famous dialogue:

"No one knows when or how I'll arrive, but I always arrive at the right time."

That's how mysterious stammering felt to him—completely unpredictable.

A RAY OF HOPE

Books had always been Harish's comfort. He searched Flipkart and Amazon for books on stammering. As a final attempt to escape the darkness, he bought S-S-Stammering by Mr. Manimaran. After finishing the book, he called the number in it and joined the Tamil Super Speakers (TSS) group on September 15, 2023.

Within two months, he attended the annual TSS conference in Yelagiri. That event changed his life.

He saw many people who had overcome stammering or were actively managing it. Some were government officers, software engineers, or successful entrepreneurs. Though not 100% cured, they had accepted their stammering without shame and practiced daily through speech drills, voice recordings, and talking to strangers.

For the first time, Harish realised that he wasn't alone, and help was available.

TRANSFORMATION THROUGH TSS

Returning to Chennai, Harish was filled with hope. He began doing the 3-minute daily voice recordings assigned by TSS and reviewing them to monitor progress. He hosted daily Google Meet calls with TSS friends and went out to speak with strangers on weekends.

In March 2024, TSS held a 10-day challenge: participants had to call a female friend or relative daily. Harish took it seriously, shared his progress, and finished the challenge successfully. He finally felt free from the invisible burden of hiding his stammer. He embraced his identity and let go of the guilt.

These efforts transformed not only his speech but also his mindset. He developed confidence, reduced his fear, and began speaking fluently. With renewed courage, he landed a job at a

Multinational Corporation (MNC) with a higher salary than before.

A PROUD MOMENT

His life's most surprising and proud moment came on October 22, 2024, International Stuttering Awareness Day (ISAD). Harish was invited to speak about stammering on Radio Mirchi. It was an unexpected opportunity to speak publicly about what he feared most since childhood.

After the interview, Harish was deeply moved, realising how far he had come—thanks to the support and practices of the TSS community.

HARISH'S MESSAGE

The TSS group helped Harish face his fears and love himself. He continues practising daily so that stammering doesn't affect his progress.

TSS offers free guidance, training, and emotional support. They expect only your consistent participation and commitment to improvement.

Harish is ready to help anyone who stammers.

"The fear we don't face becomes our limit!"

WhatsApp: 95009 26981 (Send a message first. He'll call when available)

T.K. Harish – Chennai - Tamil Nadu

Email: harish51097@gmail.com

31

FEAR? HAPPINESS? THE CHOICE OF LIFE

My name is Arun Ananthan. I was born in 1997 in Pooncholai Kuppam in Villupuram district. My father was an agricultural labourer and an electrician who passed away in a road accident ten years ago. My mother does agricultural work. I have one elder sister. Until a few years ago, we lived in poverty.

Although my parents were uneducated, they were determined to give my sister and me a good education. I was a good student, consistently ranking in the top three. The two schools I attended were extremely strict—if you didn't study, you got beaten; if you talked to other students, you got beaten. There were many reasons for punishment, and fear drove me to study hard. Every minute at school was filled with fear. I was terrified during roll calls or when teachers asked questions. I believe my schools were a primary reason for my severe stammering—along with my home environment.

My mother was also very strict. Even for minor mistakes, she would scold and threaten harshly. I was afraid of her voice. My father and my childhood friends were my only solace. My father never scolded me; even if I did something wrong, he would patiently explain it to me. On weekends, playing with friends brought joy. If they weren't available, I would happily go fishing or assist my father with electrical work.

I first realised I stammered in 2nd grade. One day, my aunt visited and said, "You study well, but you stammer while speaking!" That's when I understood I had a speech issue.

Despite my stammering, I earned a good name from all my teachers because of my academic performance. In 8th grade, there was a speech competition about AIDS awareness. My science teacher encouraged me to participate, saying it would help improve my speech. I registered, but during the 5-minute competition, I couldn't speak for more than two minutes. I was heartbroken. I wanted to share the incident with my parents that night, but something worse happened—my father, drunk, was fighting with my mother. He was calm in the morning but turned into a heavy drinker at night. I couldn't share my pain with anyone.

Though my mother was strict, she cared. When I was in 6th grade, she took me to a paediatrician about my stammering. The doctor said I would speak better as I grew up, but nothing improved.

I excelled academically, ranking third in 10th grade and fourth in 12th grade, fulfilling my parents' dreams. I then enrolled in a reputed university for a BSc in Agriculture.

My father accompanied me on the first day of college. On the way, I asked a gentleman for directions to the campus. I couldn't utter a word. As the man asked follow-up questions, I struggled to say anything. He then said, "I am the principal of that college. How did you get admission? What will you do after four years of study? You're a stammerer!" My father's face dropped in sadness. I was head down with shame. My first day of college turned into a dark one.

Despite that, I studied well. I struggled during roll calls, but I managed and completed my degree. Then came the interviews. I was rejected in my first three interviews.

Although I stammered a little in the fourth one, I answered all the questions well and got the job. I worked there for two years and then prepared for government job exams for a year. The stress from studying, the fear of exams, and unemployment worsened my stammering.

Added to that were financial struggles. With no other option, I became a Swiggy delivery boy. Every day, I had to speak to at least 50 people. The more I talked, the better I got. When I started thinking my stammering was cured, a foreign customer asked me for a hotel address. I couldn't utter a single word. That shook me. I began seriously searching for ways to fix my stammering.

Around that time, I got a good job again—but the stammering continued to follow me.

Through my friendship with Vimal Anna from Velachery, I was introduced to Manimaran Sir. After speaking with him, I gained hope that stammering could be overcome. He then added me to the Tamil Super Speakers (TSS) group. I learned more about stammering from Agniraj Anna.

As per the TSS group's advice, I practiced speaking for one hour daily and recorded three-minute voice messages on the given topics. Now, I've made significant progress. Even if I occasionally stammer, I don't worry much. I now believe that I will speak fluently one day.

My mother lives with me now. She still does small gardening tasks, but we live a much better life.

MY MESSAGE TO PARENTS, TEACHERS, AND SOCIETY

Parents and teachers—you are the biggest influencers in a child's life. When children make mistakes, explain things calmly and allow them to correct themselves. Don't hit or harshly punish them—it is violence against children. It increases fear, and they become reluctant to speak. This creates a high risk of developing a stammer. I am a living example of this.

Let children speak freely. Give every child equal opportunity.

My future plan

I plan to start an Agriculture Clinic and a Nursery Plant business.

"Let's create a world without stammering! Come join us."

K. Arun Ananthan – Puducherry

Email: ananthkumarsky@gmail.com

32

A FARMER BECOMING A UNION LEADER

Sivasankaraboopathy was born in 1982 to a middle-class family in the small town of Anamalai in the Coimbatore district. He has a younger brother. His father worked as a bank clerk for 35 years before retiring and passed away 10 years ago. His mother was a teacher at a local school, but sadly passed away prematurely when Boopathy was just 13 years old. After her passing, his father enrolled him in a hostel to continue his education.

Until age 12, Boopathy spoke fluently. However, around the age of 13, he began stammering. One of his classmates stammered, and Boopathy believes he may have subconsciously picked up the habit from him. Additionally, his mother's sudden death may have caused emotional trauma that triggered his stammering.

After he began stammering, Boopathy lived in constant fear and anxiety. He avoided speaking and would skip opportunities to talk. This deeply hurt him emotionally.

His father took him to a hospital in Coimbatore, but the doctors could not determine a suitable treatment. They advised him to speak slowly. Boopathy tried but couldn't. He even tried speaking with pebbles in his mouth, reading aloud, and undergoing painful treatments like heat applied to his tongue—all to no avail.

Despite these struggles, he completed high school and went on to earn a B. Com degree at college. He would avoid seminar classes and miss every opportunity to speak. The demon of stammering haunted him. He saw it as a disability.

HUMOROUS INCIDENTS DURING COLLEGE

Interestingly, stammering also led to some humorous events. He commuted with a school friend who studied in the same college. On the way back, instead of saying "Anamalai" (his stop) to the bus conductor, he would ask for a ticket for its fare: ₹3.50—because he struggled to say "Anamalai" clearly.

One day, a new conductor asked him, "Where are you getting off?" Unable to say "Anamalai," he blurted out "Vinayagar Temple." His friend beside him corrected him: "Aren't we getting off at Anamalai?" Boopathy quickly responded, "Yes, yes, I just forgot." Had his friend not been there, he might've ended up at the wrong stop.

Another time, he went to a hotel with the same friend. He loved Pongal but couldn't say it fluently, so he ordered *poori* instead. When his friend asked if he loved *Poori*, he lied and said yes, while feeling sad that he couldn't order the food he liked.

Though he could speak fluently with that friend, he couldn't do so with other women.

WORK-LIFE BEGINS

After graduating, Boopathy joined Reliance Communications in 2003. His job required him to speak during meetings, which he tried to avoid. One day, he was forced to speak and had to say numbers like 4 and 6, which he struggled with in Tamil. So, he cleverly used the English words "four" and "six" to get by. In this way, he often substituted words to avoid stammering and concealed his condition.

This made him feel inferior, and time passed without improvement. He struggled during conversations and avoided phone calls. Even the sight of a ringing phone would create panic. He would talk fast, omit key information, and abruptly end calls, all due to fear and anxiety.

THE TURNING POINT

He started searching YouTube for ways to overcome stammering. He came across several videos, including one in Thoothukudi that claimed it could be cured in a few months. Boopathy called him, but the man seemed more focused on money, and Boopathy didn't trust him.

Then, he patiently watched more videos and found one by Mr. Manimaran, followed by many by Mr. Agniraj. Agniraj explained what stammering is, why it occurs, whether it can be cured, how speech therapy works, and how long it typically takes. This gave Boopathy a proper understanding of the issue.

He contacted Agniraj, who explained stammering over the phone and added him to the "Stammering Tamil" WhatsApp group in December 2021. After a month of learning and watching more videos, Agniraj introduced him to the Tamil Super Speakers (TSS) group.

JOURNEY OF RECOVERY

Boopathy began speech practice every day for an hour diligently. After 200 days, he began speaking more clearly. He fully believed in the method. He practiced for three continuous years. Every day, he shared voice recordings in the TSS group. These recordings helped him feel he could speak fluently for over three minutes without stammering.

Now, Boopathy works in agriculture. TSS conducts 2-day or 3-day workshops twice a year in different towns. Since he's involved in farming, he can't attend the entire event, but he ensures he joins on Sundays. He speaks on stage using a microphone and learns new things from fellow stammerers.

TODAY'S BOOPATHY

Today, Boopathy speaks clearly and fluently. He talks confidently with everyone. Even if he stumbles on a few words, he doesn't worry. He has developed the mindset to accept his stammering, which brings him peace and eliminates fear. He no longer sees it as a disability or illness—it's just a bad habit that can be changed.

Since he began speaking well, his life has improved significantly. He is now the President of the Anamalai Tender Coconut Producers Association. He speaks confidently at many meetings and creates opportunities to speak. He happily says that he now lives life without even thinking about stammering.

PERSONAL LIFE

Boopathy married his cousin, his maternal uncle's daughter, who was already aware of his stammering, so it was never a problem. They married in 2004 and have one son, currently in his second year of college in Coimbatore. Boopathy now lives happily with his small family.

HIS GRATITUDE

Boopathy credits the Tamil Super Speakers (TSS) group entirely with his recovery from stammering. He expresses heartfelt gratitude to Manimaran Sir and Agnee Raj, who selflessly ran the group without any profit motive.

HIS MESSAGE TO YOUNG PEOPLE WHO STAMMER

He makes a sincere appeal to young people who stammer. Every youth has responsibilities—getting a good job, marrying a good partner, and providing a good education for their children. To achieve these, fluent speech is essential. He firmly believes that one can only secure a good job, find a suitable partner, and provide quality education for their children through effective communication.

Hence, he urges all young stammerers to use the TSS group effectively, overcome their stammering, and lead improved and fulfilling lives.

T. Sivasankaraboopathy – Anamalai - Tamil Nadu

Email: shankersivashanker@gmail.com

33

SOFTWARE TO BANKING

I am Anurag Mishra. I was born in 1993 in Varanasi, Uttar Pradesh, and grew up there. My father is a retired school teacher. My mother was a homemaker and passed away in 2019. I have only one elder sister. Since childhood, I have had a stammering problem, and I can't even remember when it started. In my house, apart from me, others speak well. Like everyone who stammers, my childhood and school life were filled with struggles and humiliations, making me feel like a unique child.

The children in my school would mock me by imitating my speech, saying things like "please speak slowly" and "take a deep breath." Even my family members and relatives occasionally made fun of my stammering. They turned my life into a complete hell. My older sister even advised my mother that no one would marry me if I continued to stammer like that.

My school life was similar to that of other people who stammer. When attendance was taken, I couldn't immediately say "present, sir." Others would tease me about it. Even if I knew the answers to the questions asked by teachers, due to my stammering problem, I would stand there like a mute.

Time somehow passed. 2011 I went to Agra to pursue a Computer Science and Engineering degree. I managed my stammering in the first year. But in the second year, after workshops, impromptu speaking, and presentations were introduced, my stammering became hellish.

I struggled a lot when attendance was called, often marked as "absent" because I couldn't say "present, sir." While studying in my third year of engineering college, I got Mr. Manimaran's email ID and emailed him about my attendance issues. He replied to that email, telling me to practice saying "present, sir" a thousand times daily. After several months of practicing, I made significant progress in that problem as he suggested.

After completing my third year, I participated in an industrial training program at CDAC Mohali. There, I had the opportunity to meet Mr. Jasbir Singh. (Jasbir Singh lives in Chandigarh and is an ex-stammerer. After much effort, he overcame his stammering. Even after retirement, he continues to serve the stammering community free of charge. He often conducts self-help group meetings in Chandigarh.) He invited me to his home for a meeting. In that one-hour meeting, he addressed all my doubts about stammering and guided me on various exercises and speech therapies to overcome them. That one-hour meeting became a turning point in my life. After returning to Agra, I started practicing exercises and speech training. Since there were three of us in the shared hostel room, I would go to the playground early in the morning to practice speaking.

The day came when TCS arrived at our college for campus placement drives. By the grace of God, I succeeded in all three rounds of the interview and got selected at TCS. 2015 I joined TCS as an Assistant System Engineer (trainee). Accepting my stammering, I focused on my strengths without hiding my difficulties. Even if I stammered while speaking, I didn't worry. I confidently presented during demonstrations and interacted with team members and clients.

With a strong desire to join the government sector, I successfully cleared the interview for the Senior Manager—IT position in a public sector bank in 2023 and joined in May 2023. Since it is a mid-level management role, I frequently interact with senior bank officials, vendors, and other stakeholders. I love my job and perform it with great dedication.

I want to share some of the most humiliating experiences of my life.

Once, the college chairman invited all the college toppers to discuss and plan for the upcoming college festival. At the beginning of the meeting, he asked everyone to introduce themselves. I could not utter a word when my turn came due to stammering. I left the meeting room with great shame, returned to my hostel, and cried.

On another occasion, I had to travel from Agra to Gwalior. When I reached the ticket counter, I couldn't pronounce "Gwalior." Feeling embarrassed, I left the counter without buying the ticket. Later, I wrote "Gwalior" on paper and, acting as if I were mute, showed it to the counter staff to get my ticket.

My parents have always been my most significant support. From childhood, they have never been irritated with me because of this issue. They have stood by me at every stage of my life. During my childhood, they tried everything, including giving me voice syrup (quite expensive), and explored all possible ways to help me manage this challenge. They constantly encouraged me, telling me this issue does not define me. They always reassured me that I could achieve anything in life and reminded me that many people who stammer are high achievers.

I got married in December 2019. My wife is a homemaker, and she has been very supportive of me. She is aware that I stammer occasionally, but she never makes an issue of it. From the day of our marriage until today, we have never discussed about my stammering.

In 2013, I attended a speech therapy centre for a month. There, they only taught us to prolong each sound while speaking. Inside the centre, it felt like I was speaking fluently. However, my stammering worsened when I stepped outside and faced the real world. That day, I felt extremely disappointed. An entire month of training, and the money I spent went to waste; nothing worked. Later, I realised that the only effective way to control stammering is to accept it and follow the right approach.

Now, I have a 3-year-old son. I earn a good salary in my government job, and my life is going well and happily.

To anyone who stammers, my only message is this: If you accept your stammering, you will improve your speech. Start doing this. If you do, you can manage your stammering 100%.

I want to thank Mr. Manimaran for his guidance and for making me a part of the Super Speakers group since 2014. I also thank Mr. Jasbir Singh for all his support and advice.

Anurag Mishra – Varanasi – Uttar Pradesh

Email: mishra.anurag65@gmail.com

34

A SUCCESS COMES BY STUMBLING ONLY

My name is Nishit Patel. I was born into a middle-class family on September 17, 1980, in Unjha, a town in the Mehsana district of Gujarat. My father is a farmer and also worked in a private shop. He faced many hardships from a young age because my grandfather passed away when he was still young. As a result, my father and grandmother struggled a lot to manage the family.

My family consisted of my mother, father, sister, wife, son, and daughter. I received my primary education at a school near our home, where I studied in Gujarati. I was a bright student from an early age.

I have stammered since childhood, but it didn't bother me much. Whenever I stammered, my parents would tell me, "Speak slowly, speak calmly."

I was not the only one in my family with this issue—my cousin also had the same problem.

School Days:

During school attendance roll calls, I would often feel extremely anxious. Before my name was called, my heartbeat would increase. Sometimes, I couldn't say my name on time and had to wait until the next student had responded, often making other students laugh at me.

Whenever I was asked to introduce myself in class, I would become very nervous. I tried my best to avoid situations where I had to speak.

HIGHER EDUCATION AND CAREER

Later, I entered high school. I would become highly anxious when I had to speak. However, since I consistently ranked among the top three students in school, I earned a good reputation.

After that, my father enrolled me in Bhuj Engineering College. Even there, I tried to avoid speaking as much as possible. In college, every student had to present a seminar. I would be filled with fear when the seminar date was announced. However, I faced it with courage and completed it successfully. Eventually, I graduated with a B.E. in Mechanical Engineering.

WORK EXPERIENCE

After completing my degree, I began working at a road construction equipment manufacturing company. Due to my stammering, I found it challenging to grow in my career. However, I was a hard worker, so I overcame the challenges. Later, I secured a job at a multinational corporation (MNC).

I have had several bitter experiences professionally and would like to share some of them.

One day, during an office conversation, my manager asked me a question. I started stammering and was unable to complete my sentence. Seeing this, my colleagues laughed at me. Among them were not just my coworkers but also peons and housekeeping staff. They mocked me and laughed openly. I felt highly dejected that day and couldn't even sleep at night.

Another experience I remember is when I entered my boss's cabin. Before entering, I had to say, "May I come in, Sir?" But after opening the door, I would stand there unable to utter a single word, feeling embarrassed.

Additionally, I struggled to speak during regular meetings. Even with valuable insights, I could not express my thoughts to others.

MARRIAGE

I got married in 2005. Before the wedding, my family informed my wife's family about my speech difficulty. However, they did not consider it a problem because I was academically excellent and had a good job. My wife also understood my situation and supported me.

TRANSFORMATION

To manage my stammering, I searched on Google and found Manimaran Sir's "Chennai Stammering Care Centre" website. That was a turning point in my life. The website mentioned his WhatsApp group.

I contacted him, and he added me to the Super Speakers group, where he trained me in speech therapy. From that day, I started practicing speech therapy daily at home and have remained in touch with Manimaran Sir ever since.

By understanding the nuances of stammering, I began living a better life. Because of the speech training, I found it much easier to handle speaking situations at work. My confidence increased, and even if I stammered, I stopped feeling anxious and learned to stay confident.

TODAY

I work as an Assistant Manager at a multinational corporation (MNC). Thanks to the speech therapy taught by Manimaran Sir, I have gained the courage to speak anytime, anywhere.

Speech therapy has changed my life, and I continue to practice it, which has many benefits. I will always be grateful to Manimaran Sir for transforming my life.

MY ADVICE

People who stammer should not worry. Based on my experience, I would like to offer some advice: Only by overcoming obstacles can we succeed in life, no matter what those obstacles are.

If your child stammers, I suggest not interrupting or giving advice whenever they stammer. Instead, listen carefully to what they are trying to say rather than focusing on how they are saying it. Avoid making any comments about his way of speaking.

Nishit Patel - Gujarat

Email: nishitpatel01@gmail.com

35

CHILL ICE-CREAM

I am Thiyagarajan, son of Mr. Deivasigamani and Mrs. Thulasimani, born on May 22, 1978, in Erode. I grew up there with my younger brother. My childhood was delightful. Both of us were admitted to Sengunthar Matriculation School in Erode. Until 5th grade, my stammering didn't bother me. Even my father stammered. It was only in 6th grade that I became conscious of my stammering.

For people who stammer, moments like answering roll calls, saying their name, or reading aloud in class bring immense fear. I tried various speech practices like reading aloud and practicing with pebbles in my mouth.

Although my brother used to speak fluently, he suddenly began to stammer, causing great worry.

In 8th grade, my father took me to a seven-day speech therapy session at Hotel Ajanta in Erode. There, I practiced relaxation techniques, skipping, mirror reading, and prolongation of initial sounds. The highlight was the delicious food! This happened in 1992. My father paid Rs. 8,000—a substantial amount at the time. At the end of the course, I felt very confident and spoke well. My father, who ran a mess in Erode, invited the trainer to our restaurant for a grand feast. He was overjoyed. But it didn't last. I was too young and had no one to monitor or guide me.

I was more interested in sports than in activities like public speaking or essay competitions. On the field, I would shout and run with energy, never stammering. That same passion for sports later became my biggest motivator to overcome stammering.

Back then, each home had only one telephone. To call a friend, I had to say his name and introduce myself— "I am Thiyagarajan"— which was daunting. During such calls, my heart pounded like I'd just run a 100-meter race.

12th grade was a joyful time—attending tuition and eating out were all fun. I dreamed of completing my engineering education and starting a large workshop in Erode.

In those days, college admissions were based on entrance exams and high school grades. I wasn't correctly guided, so I travelled daily to Namakkal for coaching, but mostly skipped classes. I didn't do well in the entrance exam, so my father secured a management quota seat at a reputed engineering college. He thought I wouldn't score high on the board exams. But I surprised him with 1013 marks. The college asked us to undergo regular counselling and re-select the same college, which I did. However, the management fee we initially paid was wasted. They later offered me a mechanical engineering seat for an additional cost.

In the first year, all branches study together. The second year is when you move to your department. Again, the fear returned— introductions! Until then, I studied in a boys-only school. Now, I had to study with girls. My roll number was 33. Saying it out loud was a challenge. I faced awkward moments. Friends would ask, "You speak well with us, but why stammer during roll call?" It took years to find the answer.

Engineering Mathematics II (M2) became a nightmare. I failed it and also received an arrear in practical workshops.

Thankfully, I wasn't alone—three others, including a girl, also failed. I eventually graduated with 67% and no arrears.

Two days after graduation, I attended an interview at Pricol, Coimbatore. The technical round involved using Vernier callipers and micrometres. I asked what they were for, and the interviewer sent me to the accounts department. They reimbursed my travel and meal expenses and sent me home. I felt humiliated.

Through my friend Thangarasu, I met Veeramani, a student at Anna University. At that time, E-commerce was booming, and Java was in high demand. Wherever you looked in Chennai, people carried the *Complete Reference Java* book. Training centres charged lakhs, promising job placements. Veeramani advised me to improve my English and join a small centre. I chose Radiant Centre in Adyar. Chennai's bold culture influenced me—I even wore sports shorts to class. I was passionate about Java and cleared the "Online Sun Certification"—a significant achievement.

I later worked as a Java tutor in Maraimalai Nagar, Chennai, teaching 70 MCA final-year students. They were older than I. I was nervous but asked a few questions. No one could answer, and that's when I felt like a hero. I taught there successfully for two months.

One day, my father called, crying—my mother had an accident. That call still haunts me. I rushed to Erode, praying all the way. Fortunately, she survived with only a minor disability.

Since she was bedridden for a year, my father and I managed our hotel together. After a year, my father told me to find a job matching my education. At that time, software companies were in crisis post-9/11. Many friends returned from the US, and my passion for automobiles revived. I enrolled in a three-month course at G.D. Naidu Institute and got a monthly job there for Rs. 2,500. That's where I met my mentor, Murugaiyan Sir.

I gained all my knowledge and work ethic at G.D. Naidu and Jayam Automotives. I immersed myself in R&D. To overcome my stammering, I took a six-day course in Jayanagar, Bangalore. I felt improvement for a few months, but no lasting results.

I later worked in companies like Tata Motors Pune, Mahindra Nashik, Force Motors Pune, AMW Mumbai, and Gujarat. As a Field Failure Analyst, I travelled across India (except Kashmir). However, my stammering hindered my career growth. I even tried therapy using a metronome in Pune, but the benefit was short-lived.

While working at Mahindra, my father arranged my marriage. We met the bride at a temple. I had one condition—I planned to be self-employed, not a salaried employee. They agreed. My wife's name is Visalatchi. We have two daughters—Senthamizh (11th grade, Erode) and Kavisri (6th grade, Sainik School).

In March 2015, I left a high-paying job to start my own dairy business. It began with almond milk and expanded to ice cream. I now employ 18 people. Though the struggle is real, I continue my journey with enthusiasm.

To grow the business, I joined BNI. There, I had to introduce myself and my business in 30 seconds on the mic—another challenge! Around this time, I saw an ad in Thoothukudi about curing stammering. I visited Tirunelveli, Thoothukudi, and Thiruchendur—but found no benefit. Later, I learned the person was exploiting people who stammer.

During the lockdown, I read *Redefining Stuttering*, which discussed Self-Help Groups (SHGs). That's how I discovered The Indian Stammering Association (TISA).

Through TISA, I met Manimaran Sir and Agnish Raj. I can never forget Agnish Raj's first four-hour session—it tested his patience! He explained stammering, its causes, and how/why to practice speech techniques. That's when I gained clarity about stammering. He added me to the TSS group and asked me to post a three-minute audio. It was a huge struggle.

From the next day, I started posting audio and video messages in all WhatsApp groups.

I also uploaded some videos to YouTube for a Nanayam Vikatan interview. I successfully led a workshop in Erode.

WHAT IS THE ROOT CAUSE OF ALL THIS PROGRESS? ACCEPTANCE

With my family's support, I started practicing speech therapy at home. I even attended the TSS All India Conference in Yelagiri with my family. I shared my experience with my company employees. Now, I speak confidently in many settings. I've gained many friends through TSS.

THIYAGARAJAN'S ADVICE TO PEOPLE WHO STAMMER

For new stammerers burdened by deep emotional wounds, untold mental suffering, and blocked success, the TSS group can be your sanctuary. Your sincere search may end with this group.

"Miles to go before I sleep."

– Robert Frost

T. Thiyagarajan – Erode – Tamil Nadu

Email: sridevithiyagu@gmail.com

36

LET'S STAMMER HAPPILY

The Hero of This Story: Anand

Who is this man?

What did he do?

Date: December 31, 2024

Anand, age 35 (born 1988), works as a supply chain manager at a major private bank. His job requires him to be on the phone for three hours during a 9-hour workday. Imagine stammering through all those calls—it's something a person who stammers wouldn't even dare to dream of. These aren't casual calls; he negotiates with vendors for the bank's services and materials. So, how did he gather the courage to speak so confidently?

Anand's father retired from NLC, and his mother is a homemaker. He has one younger brother.

OCTOBER 31, 2023

That morning, Anand was rushing around to get to work. He took the train and brought it to the office. As always, he responded to essential emails when he received a message from his manager asking him to come to the meeting room at 10 AM. There, the manager informed him that there would be several changes in the team, and as part of this, Anand would have to move to a different team. Anand was a bit scared but agreed.

SCHOOL DAYS: THE FIRST TWO ATTEMPTS

Anand studied in Neyveli. Even when he knew the answer, he couldn't speak up in class due to his stammer. Talking always felt like a disaster.

At age 12, he visited a speech therapist at a government hospital. The therapist recorded Anand's voice and made him listen, asking him to stretch the first syllable of words. He went for six months. It didn't help—his first failure.

Later, he heard about another speech therapist in Chennai. Anand attended a one-week program. The method was to read books slowly, loudly pronouncing the first letter and then reading the rest of the words normally. But reading from a book rarely causes stammering. It didn't help either, and he spent a lot of money unnecessarily.

COLLEGE YEARS: MORE ATTEMPTS

After finishing college in Melmaruvathur and while job hunting, Anand struggled in interviews; he knew the answers but couldn't express himself.

While in college, he visited a therapist in Coimbatore who worked with stammerers in groups. After a week-long session, Anand spoke fluently for four weeks but then relapsed. It took him 15 years to understand why. (He shares that at the end.)

Later, he saw someone else in Chennai—again, no real progress.

A friend of his father tried acupuncture, but there was no improvement.

Once, he visited someone in Salem who asked for ₹ two lakhs (in 2006). Anand ran away when he heard that amount.

ENTERING THE WORKFORCE

Anand took up a job unrelated to his field of study. He had to speak with key officials and overseas colleagues—everything felt like a distant dream. Still, he persevered and delivered.

Before marriage, he made a final attempt at therapy. He attended a two-week group session in Bangalore, which didn't help either. In 2015, he got married. Fearing rejection, he hadn't disclosed his stammering to his in-laws. His wife, an engineer in a software company, has always been supportive and never once questioned his stammering. After marriage, he stopped trying therapies for a few years.

SAMEER – THE FIRST SPARK

After being forced to switch to another team at work, Anand handled a high-priority call that went wrong—he had never stammered that badly. That moment became a turning point. This time, he wanted to try a psychologist instead of a speech therapist. He found one named Mr. Sameer. After a few sessions, Anand's fear reduced. Sameer told him he needed speech practice and recommended he look into it. Anand turned to YouTube.

TAMIL SUPER SPEAKERS – THE SPARK CATCHES FIRE

On YouTube, Anand came across Manimaran Sir's videos. He met him in person, was warmly welcomed with tea, and received an hour of guidance on how to do speech practice. He learned that Manimaran was the founder of the Tamil Super Speakers group.

Manimaran taught Anand how to accept his stammering and practice speech therapy. Anand was added to the Tamil Super

Speakers WhatsApp group, and everyone there stammered, too. Anand learned new techniques and rediscovered the same old speech therapy he learned in Coimbatore. He learned the concepts of "Little Me" and "Big Me" and understood how to let Big Me prevail.

MAY 10, 2024 – A $50,000 SAVINGS

Anand had to negotiate a significant contract with a company in Singapore. He practised repeatedly. He spoke with stammering but confidently, watching himself on camera, pausing intentionally, and breathing calmly. He explained the $50,000 cost cut clearly. After a brief silence, the opposite party agreed to discuss it with their seniors.

The next day, success was confirmed. Anand realised it wasn't just a negotiation win but a triumph over fear and self-doubt. Everyone praised him. Many more wins followed.

SEPTEMBER 23, 2024 – TOASTMASTERS

Sameer introduced Anand to Toastmasters, a club where you speak in front of 30 people on random topics. Anand joined a club near his home and won "Best Speaker" in three out of four speeches.

One topic he discussed was "3'2Au," which stood for "Three feet to Gold," a creative representation that wowed the audience.

In his first speech, he ended with: "I was stammering with fear then, I am stammering with pride now."

The hall erupted with applause.

(All his success is dedicated to the Tamil Super Speakers Group.)

ENCOURAGEMENT FROM FRIENDS

One day, while chatting over samosas with his friend, Mr. Krishnan, he asked, "Did you see a speech therapist?" You speak so well!" Anand proudly talked about the Tamil Super Speakers Group. He started making many phone calls intentionally, slowly gaining confidence. He'd often share tips with other stammerers. One friend said, "Anand Anna talks like a psychologist!"

TOASTMASTERS INTERNATIONAL SPEECH CONTEST

To compete in March, Anand had to complete two levels, which required three additional speeches in three weeks. He made it.

March 1 – Round 1: He rehearsed with friends, delivered a great speech, and won first place.

March 16 – Round 2: Facing winners from four clubs, he was the last speaker. The competition was fierce. He spoke well but secured only third place, missing qualification for the third round.

Nelson Mandela once said,

"It's not how many times you win, but how many times you rise after failing."

LESSONS LEARNED

One Sunday, Anand rested after playing shuttle with friends and reflected on the past months. Why had he progressed now and not before?

Earlier, he constantly analysed his weekly progress and stressed himself out. This time, he stopped overthinking, which removed negativity.

He was in a "do-or-die" situation, and when people reach that point, they push beyond their limits.

He made commitments:

* "I will speak with pauses."

* "I will become a great speaker."

* "I will not back down because of temporary failures."

Suddenly, a voice yelled, "Aren't you coming to eat?"—his wife, calling him from his daydream. He smiled, ate, and went to play with his son.

FAMILY

Anand lives with his loving wife and son in the third grade. His parents live with him, too.

He often wonders, "Am I 100% cured? Or should I keep pushing?" His answer: No need. His goal is to live peacefully with 90% fluency. There will be ups and downs, but worrying about them will lead to a never-ending struggle.

Even legends like Sachin and Virat have bad days. Why not Anand?

So, he practices consistently and believes he will achieve even greater success in a few years.

Until then, Anand will stammer happily.

ANAND'S ADVICE TO FELLOW STAMMERERS

* Fully accept your stammering.

* It takes months to see significant improvements.

* There will always be ups and downs—don't get disheartened.

* Don't compare last week's performance with this week's.

* Keep practising.

R. Anand Rajaram - Chennai – Tamil Nadu

Email: king.anand2008@gmail.com

37

CHENGALPATTU TO EUROPE

My name is Saravanakumar. I am from Chengalpattu, often called the "land of lakes." I was born there on July 22, 1978. My ancestral roots are from Thanjavur. My father joined the administrative department at the Thanjavur Medical College Hospital and was later transferred to Chengalpattu.

I studied at Sri Ramakrishna Mission School in Chengalpattu from nursery to 12th grade. The people of that town led simple lives. Since Chennai was nearby, many commuted daily for work. The town was well-equipped with facilities, and my parents raised me with care and values. I excelled in academics and received scholarships. My family says I spoke fluently until the third grade.

We lived in a rented house near a boy who also stammered badly. While many mocked him, I never teased him—instead, we played together and became close friends. Over time, I began stammering like him. That stammering persisted in my life. As a child, I didn't give it much importance, focusing instead on studies and sports. But when people mocked me, I began to realise my speech problem. I started withdrawing. I, once an extrovert, became introverted. Thankfully, my parents supported me.

A kind-hearted neighbour tried to help me. One asked me to read Tamil words daily, another told me to apply honey on my tongue, and someone else asked me to speak with pebbles. None of these helped much. I did benefit a bit from the reading practice, but I couldn't continue after the person moved away.

I placed third in the district in my 10th-grade exams and received medals and certificates. I was asked to speak on stage but didn't. Due to fear, I only participated in essay competitions, never in speech contests. I was interested in sports and won many prizes. My biggest mistake was avoiding speech altogether.

My stammering friend passed away. His death deeply affected me. Stammering relentlessly haunted me. In school and public, even auto drivers mocked me. I stopped talking altogether.

One painful memory: I once stood in a long queue at Tambaram station to buy a train ticket. I had to reach Chennai Central station to catch a train to Bangalore. To avoid missing it, I requested someone ahead in the queue to buy my ticket to Park Station. He agreed and took the money. When it was his turn, he bought his ticket, and when he tried to get mine, the ticket clerk asked me directly where I wanted to go. I stammered. The clerk shouted at me, saying, "You can't even talk properly! Do you want to jump the queue? I pleaded, "Sir, I have a train to catch at Central." He insulted me with harsh words. I complained to the railway manager, and that clerk was replaced. That's a different story.

Time rolled on. I was 18 years old, in 12th grade, and scored well. I dreamed of becoming a doctor, but I missed the cut-off by a few points. My parents couldn't afford a seat in a private medical college. I was heartbroken. They enrolled me at MRL Polytechnic in Manali for a diploma in Petroleum Engineering. I was not interested in this. I prepared hard again, took the entrance test, and got high marks. I joined the Government College of Engineering, Erode, for EEE in 1996. My parents struggled financially to support my education.

College days are sweet for many, but for me, they were full of challenges. I had to speak in seminars and group discussions, and I felt isolated. I got used to solitude.

In my final year (2000), I attended a Semiconductor Conference at IIT, which deeply interested me. I did my academic project in that field with the help of a professor. My project was selected as one of the best. During this time, campus interviews began. I cleared the written test but was terrified of the face-to-face interview. I saw an ad in a weekly about curing stammering in two weeks and went with my father to Coimbatore. They gave me a book to read slowly. It didn't help much. I failed the interview and felt hopeless.

Then, I saw a newspaper ad about a Semiconductor Course at IIT. I cleared the entrance, completed the course, and prepared hard for interviews. I failed in nearly 40 interviews. Finally, on the 41st attempt, I was selected by Tata.

At Tata, I worked diligently and had the opportunity to travel to the USA, Sweden, and the UK. My work was primarily technical there, so I didn't have to speak much. But I realised that technical roles wouldn't take me far. So, I pursued an MBA from IIM Bangalore, one of India's top institutions. Even fluent speakers consider it a dream! For someone who stammers like me, getting in and graduating was a matter of great pride.

Professors and fellow students supported me. Though I still stammered occasionally, I completed my MBA without significant issues.

I realised that to rise in any company, communication and leadership skills were essential—not just technical skills. My stammering remained a barrier. I joined a two-week stammering course in Bangalore. It helped a bit, but I still struggled. I limited myself to one-liner conversations at work.

In 2019, I joined Thales Group, a Defence and Aerospace Company, as a Senior Manager. By then, I had 20 years of industry experience.

My role wasn't just technical—it involved interacting with foreign clients, bringing projects to India, and expanding the business. The stress was overwhelming. I randomly searched Amazon and came across a book on stammering by Mr. Manimaran. I bought and read it. It had his phone number—I called him.

I learned about awareness workshops, communication training, self-help groups, and WhatsApp groups run by Mr. Manimaran and Mr. Agniraj. In 2023, I attended the All-India Conference held in Yelagiri, where I learned many techniques and was inspired by the stories of those who had overcome stammering. I've been part of this group for two years, regularly practising the techniques. The idea of acceptance—being open about stammering—resonated with me. I also learned about the subconscious mind.

I now practice sincerely and post regularly in the WhatsApp group, which is used constructively. This has boosted my self-confidence and led to a significant transformation.

I slowly started speaking in-office meetings. Techniques like strangers talking and pausing were beneficial. My fear and anxiety gradually vanished.

One day, my director said I had to go abroad—to Spain, Switzerland, and Germany—for business development. Friends doubted if I could handle it, but I confidently said yes. I attended 85 meetings alone in one month. The project has been approved and is now successfully operational.

Today, I confidently participate in company conferences and have won several awards. I credit this entirely to the selfless service of Mr. Manimaran and Mr. Agniraj. I'm proud to be a part of this WhatsApp group. By following their guidance, anyone can overcome stammering.

I got married on February 3, 2006, in Thiruvaiyaru. My wife is an Electronics Engineer. We have one son, Akshay Kumar, who is now in 4th grade. Until his birth, my wife worked in a private company. She then became a homemaker. I told her about my stammering before we got married. She has always been supportive.

Though I joined this group just two years ago, based on my age and the progress I've made, I offer the following advice to people who stammer:

1. First and foremost, accept your stammering openly with others. Only then can you improve.

2. Try to understand and learn as much as possible about stammering.

3. Participate in workshops conducted for the people who stammer. You'll learn new techniques, meet others, and be inspired by success stories.

4. Whatever practice you do, stick with it for years. No method will give results in just a few months.

Let's create a society free from stammering.

R. Saravanakumar – Bengaluru

Email: saravana.kumaar@gmail.com

38

COURAGE IS THE MARK OF A MAN

Prakash was born in 1981 in Pazhaverkadu, a Tamil Nadu village near Andhra Pradesh's border. His father was a fisherman, and his mother was a homemaker. He has one elder brother and one younger sister—all three siblings stammer.

After his father met with an accident, he could no longer go fishing. Instead, he started a grocery store, which he later closed due to work pressure after starting a cable TV business.

Prakash studied from 1st grade to 12th grade in a school in Pazhaverkadu. He stammered since childhood. During roll call, he couldn't say "Present, Sir" like others and would raise his hand. His teachers understood his problem and cooperated with him.

He dressed neatly for school and never picked fights. If anyone mocked his stammering, he would get angry and shout. As a result, no one dared to tease him.

Sometimes, teachers would ask each student to read a paragraph aloud. When it was Prakash's turn, he would quietly skip his spot and stand next to the student who had already read if the teacher wasn't looking. When the teacher looked at him, he would honestly say, "I stammer and cannot read aloud." Some teachers let him go, but others insisted he read anyway—those were the ones who truly helped him.

After school, Prakash wanted to study for a B.Sc., but he was admitted to a B.A. program instead. Unwilling to settle, he skipped regular college and pursued a B.A. in Tamil Literature through Distance Education.

While thinking of ways to overcome stammering, Prakash saw an ad in *Rani Weekly, a Tamil weekly, by Mr.* Balasubramanian: "Overcome stammering in one week." With his parents' permission, he attended the course in Madurai along with Mr. Manimaran.

During the course, Balasubramanian taught speech therapy and advised everyone to speak only in "Mode of Speech" (slow speech) for six months. Prakash tried this back in his village, but everyone knew him, and they mocked his slow speech. So, he couldn't implement it there.

Determined, he joined a fuel cock manufacturing company near Chennai. Everyone there was new to him, so he thought he could try slow speech. When he joined, he told the owner, "I'm not here for the salary." I have a stammer and would like to speak more slowly to improve. If you permit that, I'll work here." The owner agreed.

However, coworkers constantly mocked and ridiculed his slow speech. After enduring it for three months, he quit.

He then joined a charity kitchen in Perambur and again declared he would speak slowly. The job didn't require much communication, so after two months, he quit again.

Next, he took a one-year Leather Goods training course in Mylapore, where he met the woman, he would later marry. After completing the course, he joined a leather company in Poonamallee, but the salary was too low, so he left.

Eventually, he returned to his hometown and helped his father run the cable TV business, deciding that stammering shouldn't hold him back anymore.

Since 2002, his father has been charging only Rs. 20 for a cable TV connection. The people of the village have come together and collectively decided not to pay more than Rs. 20. His father is a very gentle person who lives by the rules of the village. He doesn't have the heart to go against the villagers.

After a few years, he started charging an additional Rs. 20 for Star and ESPN sports channels, making the total Rs. 40. Even until 2019, they were only charging Rs. 60 per connection. As a result, the cable TV business was running at a loss.

Later, as more channels were added, the fees gradually increased, and by 2019, they charged Rs. 150 per connection. However, the maintenance and operating expenses kept rising. Still, the villagers stood firm and said they couldn't pay more than Rs. 150 (and continued paying only Rs. 150 until April 2023). Meanwhile, in a neighbouring village, the cable TV operator had steadily increased the charges and, by 2023, was collecting Rs. 350 per connection.

In 2011, Prakash married the woman he loved. They now have two sons, aged 14 and 11. To improve his speech again, he joined Tamil Super Speakers (TSS) after watching Mr. Agniraj's videos and reconnected with Mr. Manimaran.

In 2020, while fixing a cable connection, Prakash fell from a height and suffered a severe spinal injury. He was bedridden for months and could walk only after a year. As a result, he was unable to participate actively in TSS activities.

He later realised he needed to take charge of the failing cable business. Though his father and brother refused to oppose the villagers, Prakash decided to speak up despite his stammer. He went door to door across 2200 homes, explaining the financial loss, stammering and being humiliated along the way.

Still, the villagers refused to budge. One day, Prakash stopped the cable service altogether. Only then did people begin to notice the seriousness of the issue. They all stopped going by boats to catch fish. The matter escalated to the police and even reached the district collector.

After hearing both sides, the collector said, "Cable operators pay high fees to broadcasters. How can they sustain if you fix such a low rate? Settle this among yourselves."

After a year-long battle, Prakash raised the subscription to ₹300 per month. The same village that once mocked him was now amazed by his courage. Not only did he go door-to-door, but he also addressed village meetings of 1000+ people, speaking for 30 minutes straight—five times.

Prakash forgot he was a stammerer in those moments, even though he stammered. He still finds this unbelievable.

Another incident: Prakash enrolled in a private training school to obtain a driver's license for a heavy vehicle. After paying ₹5000, he noticed that the instructor would abuse and hit students for minor mistakes.

When Prakash's turn came, the trainer hit him on the back of the head, angered him, though he didn't react immediately. The next day, Prakash said, "I'll drive last." When his turn came, he requested, "Please teach me without scolding." The trainer refused and told him to leave if he didn't like it.

Prakash asked for his money back. The trainer refused. Prakash went to the police, where the assistant inspector told him to adjust. Then Prakash approached the local women's association, a powerful body. The president called the police station and said, "Return Prakash's money or 50 of us will protest outside."

Within minutes, the school's owner called Prakash, apologised, said the abusive trainer was gone, and asked him to continue. But Prakash declined and got his refund.

Key Message from Prakash

When asked what advice he had for other stammerers, Prakash said:

"Sunita Williams spent 9 months in space and saw the Earth as a tiny dot. If Earth itself looks so small from space, imagine how insignificant we humans are—and our stammering problem even more so. Let go of ego, envy, and competition. Live in harmony."

He adds:

"Stammering is not even a problem. You can achieve your dreams despite it—I did."

G. Prakash – Pazhaverkadu – Tamil Nadu

Email: sobandeepan68672@gmail.com

39

DREAM IT! BELIEVE IT! MAKE IT HAPPEN!

EARLY LIFE AND CHILDHOOD

My name is Ramanathan. I was born on September 2, 1972, in Ambattur, Chennai, Tamil Nadu. My father worked as a cashier in a private company and also ran an engineering workshop. My mother was a homemaker. I was the fourth child in my family, and my birth was considered lucky by my parents. I have one elder brother and two elder sisters.

My childhood was happy. Playing with friends outside the house was joyful. At age three, I was enrolled in Johnson School, located three houses away from ours, in L.K.G. From an early age, people appreciated my speaking skills. Many praised my clear and fluent speech. However, during this time, an incident completely changed my life.

One day, when I was in U.K.G class, my mother visited relatives, staying at my grandfather's place. When I returned from school, I was shocked to find no one at home. A tenant told me my mother would return late. I felt loneliness and fear, hid behind the well, and started crying. My father, who came home for lunch, heard me crying, found me, and brought me inside.

That moment triggered my stammering (stammering started then).

Initially, my parents thought it was temporary, a common issue among children learning to speak. But it persisted. Concerned, they consulted several doctors and specialists across Chennai. Through treatment, patience, and continuous effort, my speech slowly began to improve.

EDUCATION JOURNEY

After U.K.G., I joined Model School in Ambattur, about 1.5 km away. At admission, I couldn't pronounce even the number "three" correctly and mispronounced some words. Because of that, the school moved me back to U.K.G. Despite the setback, I studied there until 4th grade.

One of my elder sisters described me as a mischievous child who often fought with siblings. My parents enrolled me in a hostel at Oxford Matriculation School, T. Nagar, Chennai, to instil discipline, where I studied up to the 5th grade. There, I ranked second among 80 students.

Later, I joined S.B.O.A. CBSE School in Anna Nagar, Chennai. I had to travel 8 km daily by public bus, and buying tickets was challenging due to my stammering. School life was tough. I was a shy student, hesitant to answer questions. Some classmates mocked my stammering, which made me mentally upset and affected my academic performance. Out of 41 students, I ranked between 25 and 28. But I was determined to prove myself. Without private coaching, I worked hard to improve on my own.

HIGHER EDUCATION AND PERSONAL GROWTH

After 10th grade, I joined Muthiah Polytechnic in Chidambaram (240 km from Chennai), where I stayed in a hostel. I felt inferior among fluent English-speaking students in Chennai, but I stood out at the polytechnic despite my stammer. Many of my peers from small towns admired my English skills. Their parents even told them to learn from me. That recognition boosted my self-confidence, improving my speech further. Polytechnic taught me independence, and having grown up, because as a child, I was always taken care of by my parents.

ENGINEERING JOURNEY

After scoring 82% in polytechnic, I joined Annamalai University to study Electronics & Instrumentation Engineering. College brought new challenges. Many Chennai students spoke fluent English, triggering insecurity again. However, a professor teaching Microprocessors encouraged me to focus on the subject instead of worrying about my stammer, which made me fall in love with the topic. I had a great circle of supportive friends who didn't mind my stammer. We're still being connected through a WhatsApp group. I completed my engineering with a First Class.

From school and college days, I've followed two principles:

* Never smoked

* Never consumed alcohol

And I continue to follow them today.

EMBARRASSING INCIDENTS

Many incidents stand out. Buying bus tickets was often embarrassing—I couldn't pronounce "Virugambakkam," and some people laughed. Kids imitated my stammer after watching me speak, but since I knew I stammered, those situations didn't profoundly affect me.

CAREER AND LIFE EXPERIENCES

In August 1995, I got my first job at NEPC Micon Ltd., Chennai, a company known for windmills and solar energy projects.

Although I continued to stammer, I learned to manage it and sought medical advice. My job involved travelling across India, including the Northeast. In 1998, my father passed away. That changed my perspective on life.

Later, I learned software development and went to Tokyo, Japan, for four months before returning to Bangalore, where I decided to settle.

In November 2002, I got married. Before marriage, I openly discussed my stammering and about my frequent travels with my future wife. Since one of her relatives also stammered, she accepted me. She followed her decision even when I reminded her again a week later.

In October 2004, I moved to the USA with my family. For four years, I worked at Citibank, New York, through Oracle, commuting from New Jersey. Later, I returned to India. Living in the USA improved my self-confidence and reduced my stammering.

From 2010 to 2012, I completed a one-year Executive Education Program in Finance at IIM Kozhikode, fulfilling a dream. I wasn't selected initially, but got in on my second attempt.

CONTROLLING MY STAMMER

In May 2018, I met Manimaran Sir, Agnee Raj, Wilfred, Yuvaraj, and others. Manimaran Sir has been an enormous inspiration, conducting free workshops for stammerers. I participated in two such workshops. Trusted by Manimaran Sir, Wilfred, and me, we were responsible for organising those two workshops, which we successfully coordinated with team coordination.

Agnee Raj has also been a powerful motivator. He and Manimaran Sir have selflessly helped stammerers without expecting money and do it at no cost.

Regular speech practice improved my fluency. However, after turning 50, health issues made consistent practice harder. Still, I follow the training given by Tamil Super Speakers to maintain my fluency.

FAMILY AND CURRENT LIFE

I have two sons—one is studying medicine in Mangalore, and the other is in 11th grade in Maryland, USA. In 2022, I returned to the USA and now work as a Data Architect in Maryland. I stammered a lot in a 2024 job interview, but thanks to my confidence and experience, I got the job and continue to perform well.

LOVING MY DREAMS

Since childhood, I've been a dreamer:

* Visiting Disneyland: In 2nd grade, my cousin sent photos from the USA. I dreamed of going too. Inspired further by V.G. Paneerdoss (VGP Golden Beach), I went to Tokyo Disneyland in 2001 and Florida Disneyland in 2004 & 2007.

* I wanted to travel outside India. So far, I've been to Tokyo, Vietnam, Canada, Singapore (for work), Malaysia, and Thailand (for tourism).

* Owning property: Inspired by playing Monopoly games during my youth, I dreamed of owning houses, and fulfilled it

* Becoming a film director: I was passionate about movies, but left that dream behind when I realised the industry didn't align with my values.

* Becoming a successful businessman: I've tried, but haven't seen significant success. Still, I've achieved many other dreams.

At 50, I returned to the USA to fulfil a promise to my wife. I still stammer but refuse to hide away—I continue to move forward.

Life comes only once, so live meaningfully. Not all dreams will come true, but some definitely will.

MY ADVICE

It'll only worsen if you're afraid of stammering every day. Instead, practice speech therapy for 30 to 60 minutes each morning, then go about your day. Don't miss out on opportunities because you stammer! Acknowledge it, speak boldly, and keep moving forward. If I had kept thinking, "I stammer" all day long, I wouldn't have been able to enjoy my dreams!

Dream, believe, and make it happen!

A. Ramanathan – Maryland - USA

Email: ramschennai10@gmail.com

40

A LOTUS SPROUTED IN THE SLUSH

Perhaps it was because we inhaled the salty sea breeze every day that the breath of education rarely touched us. Until 2013, only one doctor with an MBBS degree had emerged from our village. That same year, someone topped two Group-1 government service exams at the state level. Which one to choose? That was the moment I had been waiting for—a new beginning. That night, around 8 PM, a friend who had written the exam with me called and said, "You're the state topper!" How could I hold back tears of joy?

Whom should I tell first?

My parents, who gave birth to me?

My teachers, who moulded me into who I am?

The families who rejected me because I didn't have a government job?

The friends who eagerly awaited the results?

Or perhaps the sub-inspector who once scolded me at 2 AM near the beach while I was studying under a streetlamp for that exam, saying, "What do you think you'll become studying here at this hour?" Go home!"

Or the sea, which had supported me all these years?

In that place known for rowdyism, during my school days, I would see blood on the streets daily, not understanding the blood type, but recognising it was human blood. Perhaps that's why I grew up with various fears—blood, lizards, cockroaches, darkness. A scared man like the actor Kamal as Tenali in a movie. People who know me well say, "A lotus bloomed in the mud." Yes, I am Thamaraimanalan. Please relate my story to your own. Victory will be yours too.

EARLY YEARS AND STRUGGLES

I was born in 1985 in Triplicane, Chennai, where Lord Parthasarathy resides. I am the eldest son of a fisherman's family. My father, a fisherman who has since become a bank office assistant, is now retired. My mother was a homemaker and a part-time saree seller. I have two younger brothers—one is a swimming coach in the Tamil Nadu government, and the other is a Deputy Inspector in Indian Railways.

In UKG, a classmate falsely accused me of using a bad word, leading my mother to scold and lock me in a room. I still vividly remember crying out, "Amma! Open the door!"—a moment that possibly triggered my stammering. My mother took me to many doctors for treatment, all in vain. Wasted time, money, and hope.

Being a stammerer was like being caught between two extremes—either mute or fluent—but neither. At times, I even contemplated suicide.

STRENGTH FROM MOTHER AND MGR SONGS

Like Jijabai instilled patriotism in young Shivaji, my mother introduced me to the powerful lyrics of M.G. Ramachandran (MGR). Two songs especially inspired me. One of them was:

"If you walk into great assemblies, garlands must be placed on you." The other song given at the end of this story.

These songs lit a fire in me.

SCHOOLING AND SILENT BATTLES

In school, it took me at least 20 seconds to say my name, *Thamaraimanalan*. During lessons, when each student had to read a paragraph aloud, my heart pounded faster than a ceiling fan as my turn neared. Sometimes, I read with difficulty; often, teachers took pity on me and let me skip.

Still, until Class 10, I was the top student, excelling in studies, dance, essays, and sports. But I could never participate in speech competitions. At Raja Muthiah School, my friend Prabhu Sundar and I competed in different fields—he won the first prize in the speech competition, and I won in essay writing. I beat him academically, but he shone in speech. I always felt that void.

MY FIRST SPEECH COMPETITION

In Class 11 at Triplicane Hindu Higher Secondary School (2001), I participated in both speech and essay competitions for the first time. I won 1st place in essay—but didn't win in speech, even though I spoke well. The reason? The winners would have to talk to the Mayor of Chennai and the Local Administrative Minister of the Government of Tamil Nadu. The judges feared I couldn't do it due to my stammer.

When they told me the reason, everyone fell silent. Their sympathetic eyes brought tears to mine. I remembered Pierre de Coubertin's quote:

"The most important thing in the Olympic Games is not to win but to participate."

That moment stayed with me as a wound. Though I had won in essays, poetry, and singing, I couldn't win in speech. Would my life always be like this?

TURNING POINT IN COLLEGE

I joined a B.Sc. Nautical Science course, but later switched to B.L.M. (Bachelor of Labour Management) on the advice of an elder.

However, my family placed a condition: I had to retrieve the ₹10,000 we had paid as an advance for the B.Sc. Nautical Science course. When applying for that course, ₹10,000 had to be paid upfront. This amount would be adjusted against the annual fee if a seat were allotted. If not, it would be refunded.

Since I was compelled to get that money back, I did something for the first time—I intentionally tried not to get selected. I deliberately chose wrong answers on the entrance exam. I acted in the interview like a seasoned actor, giving a performance that would rival Sivaji Ganesan, to ensure I wouldn't be selected.

When I finally returned the ₹10,000 and handed it to my mother, I felt an immense sense of joy.

TRIUMPH AS MR. TILS

In college, I excelled in academics and curricular activities. My professors nominated me for the Mr. TILS (Tamil Nadu Institute of Labour Studies) title, which was awarded to the best male student overall. Though typically given only to final-year students, I set a record by winning it in my second year.

My professor, Mr. Sethurama Subbiah, encouraged me to participate in the speech competition. I prepared a 3-minute speech and gave a stunning performance on stage. The thunderous applause that followed was the first key that unlocked my stammering.

I continued to win prizes in poetry, cooking, rangoli, dance, and mimicry. Having already won in sports like cricket, chess, carrom, and kabaddi, I secured the Mr. TILS title. I made history. However, the final-year students boycotted the awards ceremony in protest.

CLIMBING HIGHER

I pursued my Master of Labour Management (MLM) at the same institution and won the Mr. TILS title for four consecutive years, including four first prizes in speech competitions. I topped the university in undergraduate and postgraduate studies and received the Gold Medal from the Governor of Tamil Nadu.

CIVIL SERVICE DREAM AND TSS AWAKENING

While pursuing my master's, I joined IAS coaching under the legendary Mr. Prabhakaran in Chennai. I named my children Pravasthi, Pragathi, and Prapanjan in his memory.

I left a private job at L&T in Bangalore to relocate to Chennai and focus on government exams. I even opened a tuition centre near home to help fund my studies and support others. I hired two teachers and taught from school textbooks, key for civil exams.

Between 2010 and 2013, I applied for countless government exams. I first passed the UGC-NET, became a DGM Arts & Science College professor, and then cleared several government exams, including Sub-Inspector, SBI Probationary Officer, Kalpakkam Atomic Power Station, ESI, and SSC.

However, after I cleared the SI exam, an inspector advised me to aim higher for a gazetted post, further motivating me.

TOPPING GROUP-1 EXAMS

Eventually, I topped two Group-1 level exams conducted by the TNPSC for the posts of Bursar and Assistant Commissioner of

Labour, becoming the state topper despite having low interview scores.

On October 9, 2013, I signed my appointment as Assistant Commissioner of Labour in Krishnagiri—using a green ink pen gifted to me by the sea that had once consoled me.

FAMILY LIFE AND GIVING BACK

I got married in 2013 after openly sharing my stammering with my future wife. They had no objection—I was kind and a Group-1 officer. We now have two daughters and one son.

Though I grew up in a 300 sq. ft. joint-family home in Chennai, I now live comfortably in my house in Vellore with my wife and kids. My parents still choose to stay in that same small home in Chennai.

REDISCOVERING VOICE THROUGH TSS

After joining Tamil Super Speakers (TSS), I attended a seminar in Yelagiri that reconnected me with my voice. I'm now on a journey from "stammerer" to "ex-stammerer."

People affectionately call me "Kutti MGR" (Little MGR) at my workplace. Every time I hear that, I remember the MGR's second song, which my mother taught me:

"Of the countless who have lived and died, only a few live forever in people's hearts."

D. Thamaraimanalan – Vellore – Tamil Nadu

Email: thamaraiips@gmail.com